CHER
HER STYLE PRINCIPLES

Natalie Hammond

CHER
HER STYLE PRINCIPLES

Be inspired, dress to turn heads

CONTENTS

INTRODUCTION 7

14
DRESS TO THE BEAT OF YOUR OWN DRUM

30
HONE A SIGNATURE (AND SPECTACULAR) SILHOUETTE

46
DON'T BE AFRAID TO EMBELLISH

62
SHAKE UP YOUR MAKE-UP

82
FIND THE COLOURS THAT MAKE YOU FEEL FABULOUS

106
LOVE YOUR ROCK 'N' ROLL LEATHER

120
DOUBLE DOWN ON DARING DENIM

132
EMBRACE AN ALTER-EGO

148
CHOOSE EYE-CATCHING ADD-ONS

168
EXPERIMENT WITH BIG-PERSONALITY PRINTS

CONCLUSION 186
PICTURE CREDITS 187
REFERENCES 188

'All of us invent ourselves. Some of us just have more imagination than others.'

CHER

INTRODUCTION

In 1982, Cher performed at Caesars Palace, Las Vegas, and promoted a one-night-only TV special to be aired the following year. The poster left fans in no doubt about whether or not they would be getting their money's worth: 'Sexy, Sizzling, Sensational Cher in an electrifying one-hour concert special!' Quite the billing. Cher did not disappoint, delivering a fever dream of barnstorming covers and showgirl costumes, the latter outrageous in their brief proportions and blinding sparkle.

For her first number, 'Could I Be Dreamin'' (1980), Cher is crowned with a headdress more than two metres across. The almighty plume of fire-coloured feathers wobbles above a skimpy red-and-silver dress shooting up at the hip bones. Viewers are used to certain glamazon tendencies from her prime-time era on TV, but this is something else, an extravaganza of camp involving not just outfit changes but wig transitions in front of the audience's eyes. After the opening tune segues into 'Signed, Sealed, Delivered (I'm Yours)' (1970), three men gather around Cher. 'Hello, my darling,' she purrs at the chosen one kneeling in front of her. 'Never a nasty little frown on his face,' she continues, as he deftly fastens the waist of her next get-up while motorboating her stomach. And it gets better. For 'Those Shoes' (1979), Cher rides onto the stage on a gigantic mule sandal, gyrating at the curve of its heel before sliding down its sole and through its peeptoe. For anyone watching, it was a parallel universe of sequins, hair and shoes – sexy, sizzling, sensational and one hundred per cent Cher.

Cherilyn Sarkisian was born with showbiz in her blood. After watching two movies as a little girl, *Dumbo* and *Cinderella*, she knew that she needed to be part of the acting world. She even practised her autograph from the age of 11. 'I set out to be famous!' she said simply during a 2018 interview with Philip Galanes from the *New York Times*, adding, 'I set out to be Cinderella.' And in fact, her story wasn't entirely dissimilar from her idol's rags-to-riches character arc.

INTRODUCTION

Cher was born on 20 May 1946. Her father, John Sarkisian, was largely an absent figure, despite being married to her mother, Georgia Holt, three separate times. Their daughter's early fascination with fame was inherited from Holt, a jobbing actress who lost out on the part of a lifetime to Marilyn Monroe (as Angela Phinlay in *The Asphalt Jungle*). Dyslexic and disinterested in school, Cher left home at 16, which is when she crossed paths with Sonny Bono, the man who moulded her early career, sculpting a marketable star (and his future wife) out of an ingénue with a vocal register so deep that people initially mistook it for a man's. 'I Got You Babe' (1965) was a turning point for their double act Sonny & Cher, an iconic record that eventually became the outro number of *The Sonny & Cher Comedy Hour*, the couple's reinvention as variety-show hosts after their cool-factor as musicians waned in the late sixties. When they parted ways professionally and romantically, Cher rebounded with a new TV show on CBS, *Cher*, the mononym that she'd legally adopt four years later, dropping 'Sarkisian', 'Bono' and any subsequent last name that might follow. Wearing costumes by Bob Mackie, whose designs are a sacred part of fashion history, Cher's radiance was finally set to full beam.

Cher's style legacy could fill several books. Her wardrobe has been a talking point since time immemorial, mentioned in almost every one of her talk-show appearances, often slyly and rarely in passing, with interviewers lingering on its finer points with a breathtaking lack of subtlety that, quite honestly, mirrors her greatest outfits. On 13 November 1987, Cher appeared on the *Late Show with David Letterman*, reuniting with her ex-husband Sonny. After wearing a spangled body stocking for a rousing performance of 'I Found Someone' (1987), Cher settled into an armchair for the interview. 'You sounded great,' said Letterman. 'What the hell were you wearing exactly? Was there a fire at the hotel or something?' She was undeterred, landing a few jabs of her own later in the segment. (When Letterman poked fun at Sonny, pointing at his bare abdominals in some old promotional material from the days of Sonny & Cher, Cher didn't miss a beat: 'Show us your stomach, David.') Because despite the gawking and negative attention it sometimes garnered, Cher refused to dial down her look for anyone, including the Academy of Motion Picture Arts and Sciences, who balked at her young boyfriends and barely-there clothes as she attempted to cross over into Hollywood. She wanted to be taken seriously, hoping to fulfil her adolescent dream of acting, but on no one else's terms but her own.

Of course, the joke's certainly not on Cher. Not only has she produced 27 studio albums to date and landed a number-one hit in the charts for six decades straight, but she's also the recipient of three Golden Globes, one Emmy, one Grammy, and one Academy Award. She's also been celebrated by the prestigious Kennedy Center Honors (2018), as well as receiving an induction into the Rock & Roll Hall of Fame in 2024. Cher has built a career off the back of a masterful ability to reincarnate, shifting from pop singer to prime-time star to leading lady to dance-anthem diva, adopting different clothes for different eras. Despite the accolades, Cher's been in and out, up and down. During a 2018 sit-down with Gayle King, she even joked that she'd finally won an Academy Award, the pinnacle of achievement by anyone's standards, only to wind up doing infomercials. What's remarkable is that she's managed to weather the outs with comeback after comeback, never missing a beat when there's an opportunity for a new chapter. She's TV gold. A Broadway star (both treading the boards herself and providing material for her very own stage biopic, *The Cher Show*). An arena legend. And, undoubtedly, a fashion icon.

Cher's attitude to getting dressed marked her out from the beginning of her career. She's a risk-taker, always pushing for something that would cause nothing less than shockwaves; she has never stuck to rules or to one way of

INTRODUCTION

making an impact. As she once told *FASHION Magazine*, 'The thing I love about style is that it is continually evolving. I don't believe I've ever had a uniform.'

That might be true, but it doesn't mean she doesn't rely on certain style principles, pulling out silhouettes and shades calibrated to always hit, never miss. In these pages, you'll learn how to distil some of those signature moves, channelling their audaciousness while always making them your own.

DRESS TO THE BEAT OF YOUR OWN

DRUM
DRUM
DRUM
DRUM
DRUM

'Until you're ready to
look foolish, you'll never
have the possibility
of being great.'

CHER

When Cher arrived at the Oscars in 1986, she was making a very particular statement. She had finally conquered Hollywood, with one nomination already under her belt for *Silkwood* (1983), a critically acclaimed drama co-starring Meryl Streep. But three years on, not only had she been passed over for her performance in *Mask* (1985), but she also was bristling at not being considered a so-called 'heavyweight' actress by the Academy. Cher being Cher, she pulled a number on its overlords, who had deigned to ask her to present the award for Best Supporting Actor, issuing a specific brief for the ceremony. Speaking to the *New York Times Magazine*, whose interview ran 18 months later on 18 October 1987, Cher said, 'I wasn't going to go at all. And then they asked me to present, these people who had just said, "No, you can't be one of us." I thought, *Okay, you can go in a simple black dress and be just like everyone else.* But then I decided, I'm going to remind them of what they don't like about me.'

She came and conquered, a jet-black mohawk erupting above her regal head like a lion's mane, towering over Don Ameche, the actor to whom she presented the gold statuette. A toned foot of flesh was visible between her latticed crop top and beaded column skirt, its zig-zag waistline drawing the eye down from her navel, *always* a source of controversy for the omnipotent censors during her days on CBS. (In the same year, Geraldine Page took home Best Actress, posing after the fact in a magisterial but modest velvet cape. Cher also wore a cashmere shawl, incidentally, but naturally it did little to counter the effect of the sky-high feathers and tantalisingly bare skin.) Cher stood at the podium, gazing magnanimously at the audience and said, 'As you can see, I did receive my Academy booklet on how to dress like a serious actress.' The score at the close of the ceremony was Cher: 1, Academy: 0.

Cher didn't need to be given a handbook on how to dress. She wrote the handbook on how to *dress up*. The Oscars outfit might have gone down in history, but it was just one of many of Cher's looks that constituted A Moment. She always dressed to the beat of her own drum, operating entirely outside the trend cycle and refusing to entertain anyone else's idea of what she ought to wear, however much it affected her chances in Hollywood.

One glance at her album covers tells you all you need to know. They're a snapshot of a life that's been lived with a glorious sense of escapism when it comes to dressing up. Two stand out. For *Take Me Home* (1979), Cher was dressed as a fantastical warrior princess, with her version of high-fashion armour, not to mention a headdress shaped like an outstretched pair of dragon wings, all rendered in gold. This album of disco anthems was a hit with listeners, which sadly wasn't the case for *Prisoner* (1979), which came out the same year. Its cover, however, was incendiary. Pictured in front of a column with an urn by her feet, Cher appears naked apart from chains wrapping her wrists, thighs and ankles. Look closely and you'll see how each length of links is draped just so, almost creating a skirt. Obviously, this wasn't left to a prop master but orchestrated by the maestro himself, Bob Mackie. And until you understand this man's sense of invention – as well as his indefatigable work ethic and a soaring ability to dream big – you won't understand Cher.

Together, they made nothing short of magic after meeting just as the sixties, a time of free love but comparatively modest fashions, was about to give way to the seventies, a decade where you dressed up. And as we've already seen, nobody did that quite like Cher.

DRESS TO THE BEAT OF YOUR OWN DRUM

MEETS

Mackie might have dressed the greatest of stars over the years, including Judy Garland, Mitzi Gaynor, Carol Burnett, Diana Ross, Barbra Streisand and Tina Turner, but he arguably had the most enduring relationship with Cher. She was his muse; he was her co-creator. 'This might sound strange to some, but of all the men in my life, Bob Mackie has been one of the most important, hands down,' she wrote in the afterword to the book *The Art of Bob Mackie*.

Mackie cut his teeth with the undisputed doyenne of costume design, Edith Head, providing sketches for iconic movies like *A New Kind of Love* (1963), which scored a nomination for the Best Costume Design (Color) Academy Award. He also crossed paths with Marilyn Monroe, drawing the sketch for the sensational 'naked' dress she wore to serenade President

John F. Kennedy. The dress was designed so that, under the stage lights, those extraordinary curves were dusted with rhinestones as she delivered her legendary rendition of 'Happy Birthday'. Eventually, TV came knocking. Mackie racked up credits on *The Judy Garland Show*, *Alice Through the Looking Glass* and *The Carol Burnett Show*, the latter featuring a long-haired husband-and-wife duo, Sonny & Cher, who'd got a hit under their belt but were struggling on the nightclub scene having fallen out of favour with the 'in' crowd. According to legend, Mackie met his future muse backstage, where she was admiring the beadwork on a gown of Burnett's. A straight-shooter from the off, Cher wasted no time, telling the designer she wanted to wear something like that one day. In 1971, her wish came true: *The Sonny & Cher Comedy Hour* got its own slot on CBS.

Because of his relentless schedule on *The Carol Burnett Show*, Mackie only signed on to design costumes for Cher, zipping between the studios through a handily located men's toilet. The rest is history. In his hands, Cher became one of the best-dressed women in America, with the kind of costumes – plunging, glittering, mesmerising – that made the average viewer dare to dream. Mackie has been by her side ever since, designing costumes for her solo venture Cher, reboots (the short-lived *The Sonny & Cher Show*), albums, magazine covers, red-carpet triumphs and the musical theatre extravaganza on Broadway, *The Cher Show*.

She, meanwhile, never stopped trusting his judgement. On 11 April 1988, Cher was poised for victory at the Oscars for her role in *Moonstruck* (1987), and filmed a segment beforehand that would air on the night as part of *The Barbara Walters Special*. Sitting on a plump cream sofa, hair permed and feet curled beneath her, with her spidery limbs clad in black sweats, she dished on the dress she had planned – 'beautiful' and 'skimpy', words that would inspire delight from some, eye rolls from others. 'Then he designed this very beautiful, what he called, wrap to go over it. I said, "No, no, no, I don't want a wrap. I want a black motorcycle jacket. And I want you to bead it exactly the same as my dress. Can you do that?" He kind of gulped and said, "Well, that's very interesting, Cher." His face fell to the floor.'

Cut to the red carpet, and she's wearing the dress she described, her lithe body draped in beads which beam as brightly as her smile, but there's no leather jacket in sight. Instead, she's wearing the wrap. Evidently, she listened to Mackie. As Cher stood on the winner's podium, she said 'I don't think that this means that I am somebody, but I guess I'm on my way.' And Mackie was undoubtedly one of the reasons why, surviving the ups and downs, she got there against the odds.

HOLD THE REINS OF

The average person doesn't have a Mackie, a genius pulling the strings behind the scenes to ensure every outfit sizzles. But you can still cultivate a wardrobe that reflects your personality, yet also pushes you out of your comfort zone. Because while you should never wear – or, crucially, buy – anything that doesn't feel like 'you' there and then, it's fun to occasionally throw a curveball. Just remember: the only person's opinion that matters is your own.

When Cher was speaking about her dress for that auspicious night with Barbara Walters, she explained why she felt so passionately about the leather jacket, although, obviously, she changed her mind at the final hour. 'I feel like that's really me,' she said. 'I know it's not "appropriate" but, to me, appropriate seems very misplaced in our society. I believe if you look at the Reverend Jimmy Swaggart, or if you look at Ronald Reagan, or if you look at all of these people who are supposed to be the pillars of our society, and if you look at the way they dress, well, they dress very "appropriate".

YOUR OWN WARDROBE

But I question their interiors. And I don't question my interior. My exterior is unimportant.' Maybe she wore clothes that scandalised, but she didn't set out to be scandalous; she was simply trying to be herself, a person that just happened to be comfortable holding court in turbo-charged sequins with hair up to there.

Perhaps you already know your signature look, in and out and back to front. Or maybe you find the act of getting dressed a daily struggle, less a chance for self-expression and more a chore on your way to leaving the house. You won't be able to find your personal style overnight. A way to start the 'journey', however, is by taking stock of what's already in your wardrobe, donating anything that no longer fits and making a mental list of gaps that need to be filled. Once you've cleansed, so to speak, you can ask the hard question: 'What do you want your clothes to say about you?'

Cher's wardrobe proves that she is a person who finds pleasure in dressing up, a person who seizes the day as if it could be her last on earth. And if there's one legacy her fearless style has gifted to mankind, it's the naked dress. Let's begin with a decided bang and start there.

PUT YOUR OWN SPIN ON THE NAKED DRESS

The naked dress has taken on a life of its own in the twenty-first century, becoming so customary on the red carpet that it's not so much shocking as standard practice. It was a different story in the seventies. Because while the decade might have been characterised by sex and sequins, a tide of hedonism crashing over popular culture which culminated in the opening of Studio 54, it was still considered outré to show certain body parts in public. Cher wore the original naked dress – possibly not the first but certainly the best in the genre – a 'gown' that looked as if she was wearing beads and only beads, made by Mackie (see page 48). It was so eyebrow-raising that when it landed on the cover of *Time*

– Cher's limbs composed in a curvaceous position as she gazed into the camera, quite a departure for a hard-news periodical which, in the same year, ran covers of Mother Teresa, J. Edgar Hoover and Ronald Reagan – it was actually pulled from newsstands in Tampa, Florida. I'm not suggesting you wear beads and only beads to your next party, but leaning in to the idea of a birthday suit is no bad thing if you want an introduction to dressing more like Cher. Try harnessing a little of her wardrobe's daring-do for your next escapade. Luckily, you can do a naked dress without being naked. Seek out garments that utilise the reveal-and-conceal nature of see-through fabrics: a flaring skirt made of peekaboo lace which you can slip over high-waisted knickers; or semi-sheer trousers which often come with an opaque panel for practicality. In the naked-dress arena, you've got diaphanous silk-georgette gowns whose whisper-thin layers are a modest take; lace-trimmed slips which shoot up at the calf and down at the décolletage; or ruched jersey dresses which cling around the hips so that every fabulous curve is on show.

HONE A SIGNATURE

(AND SPECTACULAR)

SILHOUETTE

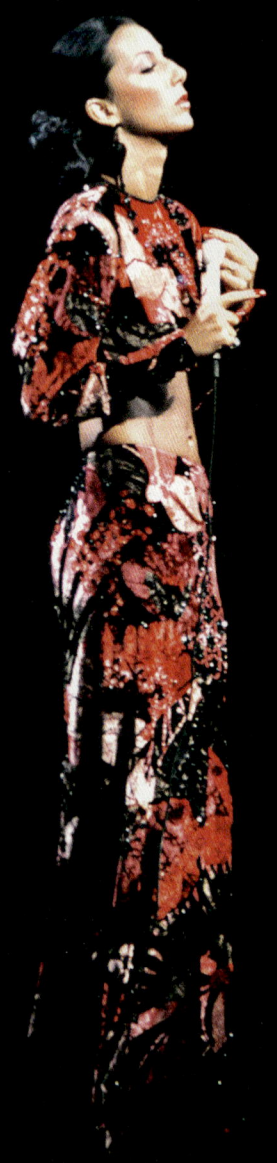

'I met her on *The Carol Burnett Show* in '67 – the first year we did it. She had a beautiful body. It was a beautiful shape – beautiful arms and just the most beautiful armpits!'

BOB MACKIE

After Cher's solo show got the green light, premiering on 12 February 1975, one part of her anatomy would eventually become a weekly talking point – if not for viewers at home because of certain post-production trickery, then certainly in the studios of CBS. Her navel. 'I was the first person to ever show my belly button on TV,' Cher told *After Dark* magazine's Brant Mewborn four years later in February 1979. This was a problem because of the so-called Family Hour, a 60-minute slot every Sunday in which networks were obliged to ensure their content was appropriate for every generation. Cher's spin is somewhat more colourful. 'Someone at CBS came up with the idea that my belly button was corrupting American morals. They confiscated pictures of me in which my navel was showing and tried to force me to keep it covered. But the censors' argument never made sense. I was already showing my navel on *The Sonny & Cher Comedy Hour* for years and people loved it.'

It was true. Cher's belly button had been a frequent guest on her and her then-husband's show, which ran from 1971 to 1974, as much a part of the furniture as the comedy sketches, starry acts and rather spiky repartee between the married hosts. For Cher, it had been a baptism of fire in the kind of comedy (and gruelling schedule) that set the stage for her own variety show, which, as we know, is where the censors really had their work cut out.

Cher's costume department had a budget of $30,000 an episode, which roughly translates as $175,000 today, an eye-watering sum and a sign that her wardrobe was expected to deliver ratings (Nielsen Media Research ranked the show 23rd for the 1974–75 season with a rating of 21.3, narrowly beating *The Carol Burnett Show*, which came in at 29 with a rating of 20.4). The show was an unparalleled feat of engineering and exuberance from the beginning, with the kind of outfits that made her not so much a pin-up as a style icon, as she patented a very particular silhouette, slinky to the point of making her look statuesque, despite the fact that she's an only slightly-above-average 1.71m tall.

On Sunday nights, viewers would immediately be rewarded for tuning in to *Cher* with a musical number that would start in a pitch-black studio, Cher's figure illuminated by a spotlight, tantalisingly draped in a ruffled cape or a feathered wrap which covered her body from top to toe as a disembodied voice intoned, 'Ladies and gentlemen... Cher.' On 16 March 1975, the camera panned forward as she sang the opening to 'Friends' (1973), Bette Midler's hit. As soon as she reached the famous refrain, she ripped off a fringed cape festooned with flowers to reveal a satin gown the colour of an egg yolk, shining as she danced forward on a moving ramp to give the audience a glimpse of that perfectly honed stomach.

HONE A SIGNATURE (AND SPECTACULAR) SILHOUETTE

Cher always set out to entertain her audience with the new guard of rock 'n' rollers, as well as the brightest lights of comedy, pop, jazz and R&B. She succeeded with line-ups that included Elton John, Labelle, The Jackson 5, David Bowie, Ray Charles and Tina Turner. What she also did was create an hour of escapism with her extraordinary wardrobe, which would have influenced people at home to wear (or dream of wearing) the fantastical silhouettes that appeared week in, week out.

You might not have the opportunity to stage a 'reveal' the next time you're out with friends, but what you can easily do is copy the silhouettes of Cher, borrowing those signature proportions, both soaring and sweeping, that gave her wardrobe such flair. And note: if 'soaring and sweeping' are outside your comfort zone, what you'll learn in this chapter is how to lean in to silhouettes that make a statement, whatever that looks like to you (an exaggerated shoulder, a nipped waist, an elongated leg – you name it).

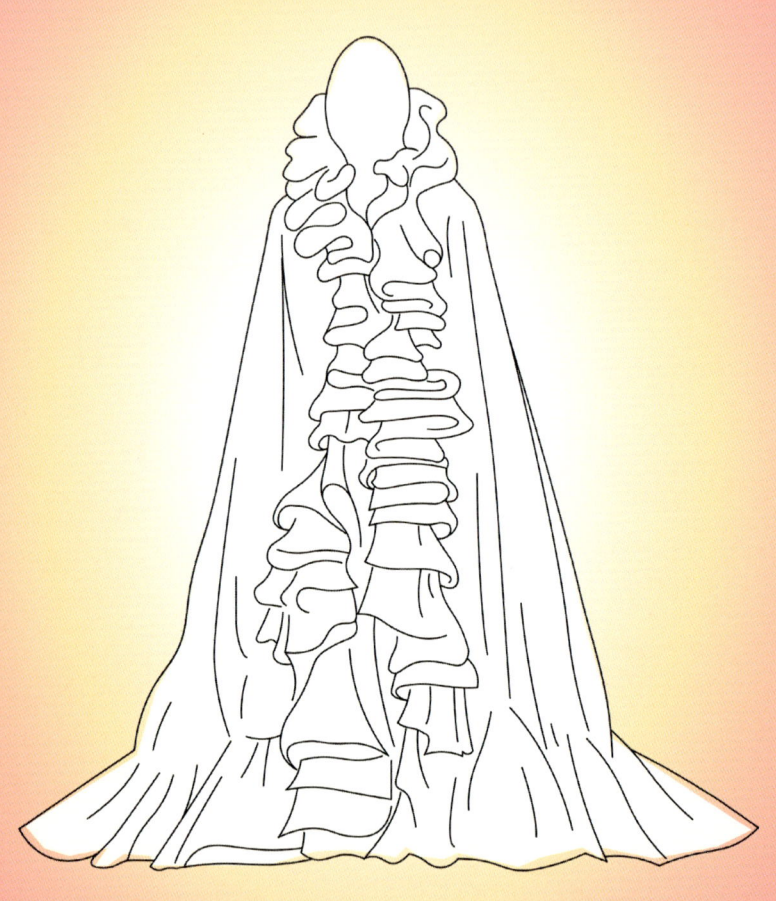

'I could hardly take a bad picture, and all my clothes were fabulous and I loved them – and I spent pretty much all my time naked.'

CHER

TOP OF THE CROPS

Cher's body often prompted specific queries about her weight and measurements from her studio audience – and she wasn't coy when it came to celebrating its proportions. At 1973's Academy Awards, a decade before she would make her first moves in the world of acting, Cher's stomach was central to her outfit, a high-necked blouse with billowy sleeves which left a fantastically toned foot of skin on show. It was a tried-and-tested formula that was to be repeated at the Oscars in 1986 with another high-fashion take on the crop top, the year she was snubbed for her role in Mask (big mistake). Often styled with a relatively modest neckline for balance, Cher became top of the crops, often wearing a criss-cross design encrusted with beads to elongate her torso. And that's exactly how you, too, can work a cropped silhouette into your wardrobe: by choosing a blouse that compensates for its brevity with details like an elegant turtleneck or a voluminous sleeve. Another trick is to pair your brief top half with a high-waisted bottom half to minimise the amount of skin that's actually on show, which can be the merest sliver if your trousers are sufficiently high-rise. Cher, however, was comfortable with showing more than a sliver, thank you very much, and used to pair her crop tops with another silhouette that became a signature: fluid maxi skirts.

HONE A SIGNATURE (AND SPECTACULAR) SILHOUETTE

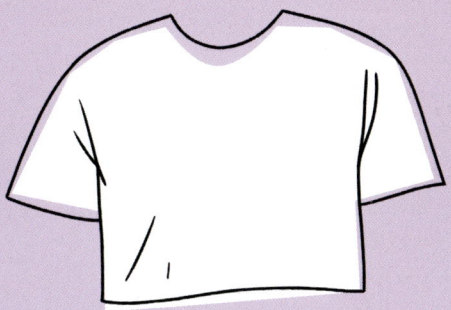

CROPPED WHITE TEE

High-waisted chinos	Denim maxi skirt	Wide-legged black trousers
+	+	+
Red suede loafers	Slouchy knee-high boots	Oversized cream blazer
+	+	+
Silver hoop earrings	Chunky gold ring	Brown leather sandals

ANKLE-SWISHING SKIRTS

Cher's take on the maxi wasn't a ball gown-style skirt that girlishly fanned out from the waist. It was very grown-up, a slender column with a waistband just below her navel, a fit that stayed close to her frame with a floor-sweeping hemline. The effect was mesmeric, cleverly making her legs appear just as languid as her torso. This was the early seventies but, interestingly, this silhouette hit its stride once again in the nineties, when the cult of minimalism edged out the shoulder pads and perms of the eighties.

The maxi skirt has shape-shifted almost as much as Cher, which is no bad thing. There are straight-up-and-down skirts made of knitted fabrics which fall with a certain amount of fluidity; pleated skirts with slightly more flare; denim skirts which hit the ankle and come with a strategically positioned slit at the side; leather skirts which emulate the column style of Cher's. If you've never dipped your toe into the world of maxis, preferring the middle ground of a just-below-the-knee skirt, I would suggest trying a range of different brands in a department store. Take a pair of heeled leather boots with you if possible (the extra fabric means that a boost in the height department will immediately make your maxi look the part). Cher obviously wore hers with crop tops, but they can just as easily slot into a modest frame of mind with a crew-neck jumper or thin-gauge polo neck worn under a slightly undone button-down shirt.

HONE A SIGNATURE (AND SPECTACULAR) SILHOUETTE

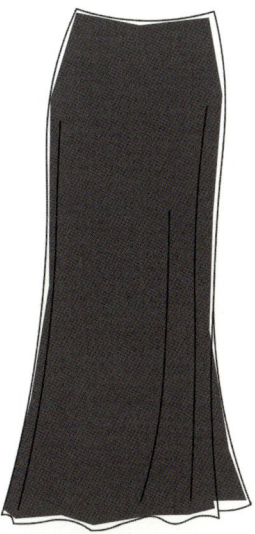

BLACK SILK MAXI SKIRT

Cream shirt	White vest top	Off-white T-shirt	Black tunic-style top
+	+	+	+
Cord necklace	Denim jacket	Fringed suede jacket	Studded belt
+	+	+	+
Black ballet pumps	Gladiator sandals	Retro trainers	Black leather sandals

FIND YOUR FLARE

When Sonny met Cher, she was a 16-year-old on the cusp of womanhood, a girl he knew could make them both stars. Cher mostly went along with it; he was 27, a bonafide singer-songwriter running in the same circles as Phil Spector, who eventually landed her a credit as back-up singer on iconic anthems like 'Be My Baby' (1963). But when it came to what they wore, Cher took charge, dressing herself and her future husband, and favouring one item that was the height of sixties fashion: flares. Cher's bell bottoms were slender to the knee then kicked out, often rendered in burnished sequins or bold stripes. These are trousers guaranteed to get you noticed, but if you'd prefer a slightly more subtle approach, avoid patterns or anything embellished, instead choosing a loose-fit corduroy trouser with an ever-so-slight flare or a pair of gently sloping jeans, high on the waist and wide at the hem. Then again, turning heads is part of the fun, so if you want to try a statement trouser, go right ahead. Cher certainly would.

HONE A SIGNATURE (AND SPECTACULAR) SILHOUETTE

BROWN CORDUROY FLARES

Grey cashmere jumper	White vest top	Cream polo neck
+	**+**	**+**
Snake-print cowboy boots	Studded denim jacket	Brown oversized blazer
+	**+**	**+**
Red beaded necklace	Black ballet pumps	Black leather clogs

DON'T BE AFRAID TO

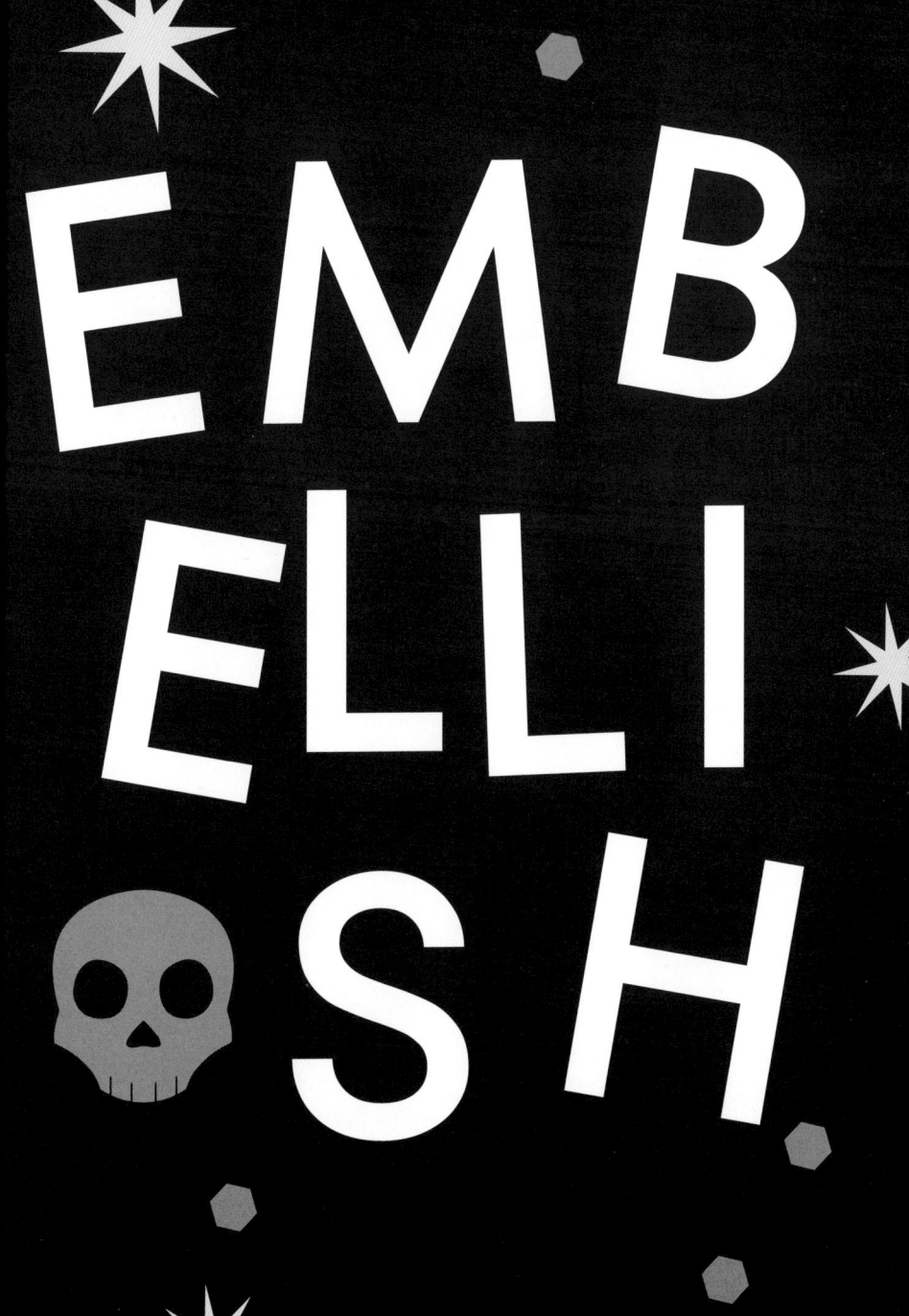

'More elaborate. More covered in diamonds. More glamorous. More peekaboo.'

BOB MACKIE

Time has a legacy of truly great newsstand covers, the kind that immortalise the glory, ignominy or hope of a specific moment. On 17 March 1975, that honour went to Cher. Photographed by Richard Avedon, an icon himself whose subjects included Marilyn Monroe, Audrey Hepburn, Elizabeth Taylor, Prince and Tina Turner, Cher appeared in an outfit that outraged certain members of the public (to say nothing of her bosses at CBS).

She looked naked at first glance, wearing a gossamer-thin gown made from a fabric called souffle. It was the same colour as her skin and sewn with silvery beads which shot up and down her body in strategic comets, while the elbows and hemline burst with snow-white feathers that only seemed to enhance the fact that she was essentially wearing not a lot. It was an immediate sensation, despite the fact that she'd already taken it for a spin at the hallowed Met Gala. Mackie still remembers the brouhaha. 'It created a lot of hubbub. In those days, *Time* reserved its cover for world leaders or someone who invented something important, like a vaccine. The newsstands sold out of it immediately, and some cities even banned it – funny, considering how some stars can barely keep their clothes on today,' the designer says in *The Art of Bob Mackie*. Cher wasn't a world leader, but she was the inventor, the poster woman, of the super-charged glamour that would define the decade's approach to getting dressed after the comparatively staid fashions of the sixties. Modest was out, megawatt was in, and Cher was leader of the pack when it came to the kind of embellishment that stopped traffic.

Whether it's beads, feathers, sequins, fringe, studs or a combination of the above, Cher and embellishment have gone hand-in-glove since the early seventies. And we aren't just talking about a finishing touch, a final dusting calibrated to dazzle. In many cases, the embellishment *was* the outfit. At 1974's Grammy

Awards, Cher wore a kaleidoscope of 'butterflies' – and little else. A bikini-style top with a halterneck string tie featured a pair of sequinned wings in ice-blue and pearlescent lilac, while another insect settled just above her left ear. Joking backstage with legends like Stevie Wonder, who also repped embellishment with an embroidered jacket that featured stitched flowers on its shoulders and cuffs, Cher had found her spangled mojo after separating from Sonny. And she never lost it.

On the Living Proof: The Farewell Tour, which lasted for three smash-hit years from 2002 to 2005, Cher's wardrobe was a progression of steadily more embellished looks, from crystallised balcony tops with fringes of cubic zirconia, to fabulous hareem pants, black and beaded, which furiously twinkled under the stage lights. One headdress even dripped with silver filaments which recalled one of the session photoshoot looks for *Prisoner*, where she was transformed into a butterfly, wearing nothing except for a beaded wig that fell strategically over her body, naked save for a pair of wings.

That particular look was by Mackie. His gift for shimmering and altogether stupendous design meant his charge became the queen of a kind of embellishment that can only be described as extraordinary. However, it's important to remember that while what you're wearing can shine, it should never eclipse you. As Cher told *Time* magazine way back when she appeared on the cover that shocked America: 'I wear my clothes; my clothes don't wear me.'

HOW TO LIVE A MORE EMBELLISHED LIFE (EVEN IF YOU'RE NOT CHER)

We don't all have a calendar of red-carpet events, talk shows and film premières to attend. If we did, embellishment would be part of everyday life. But your wardrobe still deserves a little drama. Don't forget, embellishment is more a state of mind than anything else. It shouldn't be saved for once in a blue moon. Cher's take on studs, beads and crystals was always full-throttle. Yours doesn't have to be. Instead, keep reading to discover how to bring that special brand of 'wow' to whatever you're wearing.

STUDS

As well as sparkle, Cher has another favourite embellishment that's less showgirl and more straight-up rock 'n' roll: studs. Germany's *Wetten, dass..?*, a TV programme which has been on air since 1981, came calling in November 2023. Cher graced the stage, singing an alt-classic 'DJ Play a Christmas Song' (2023), wearing a lace bodysuit with a pair of trousers whose surface was studded with metal rivets, some of which revealed peekaboo circles of skin. Cher's Christmas album might have been the topic of conversation, but her outfit was the opposite of a traditional festive get-up.

Such an embellished bottom half might be too much for most of us, but the good news is that studs couldn't be easier to incorporate into your wardrobe in a way that's subtly head-turning. A black studded belt is the easiest way to add a little something extra to low-rise jeans or the hips of a knitted slip dress – and vintage shops are probably the easiest place to look for a belt whose leather is a little aged, giving it that lived-in look. Eyelet-embellished shoulder bags are a great way to add edge to whatever you're wearing – although it might be too much of a good thing to pair one with a leather jacket, FYI.

Ballet pumps embellished with silver press studs or eyelets, meanwhile, have experienced a boom over the past few years thanks to luxury brand ALAÏA, whose flats reached cult status in 2022. Similar iterations have since trickled down to almost every high-street brand, and they're especially good at dressing up a lo-fi outfit of baggy jeans or tailored black slacks.

BEADS

When Cher wore beads, they weren't so much an embellishment as the essence of her entire outfit. The *Time* gown was sprayed onto her body so that each bead looked as if it was stuck to her skin, creating an illusion with the invisible fabric that was almost as shimmering as it was salacious. The courage to wear beads and only beads, as we've seen, might be one hurdle that many of us are too shy to contemplate. But Mackie made a very good point when he revisited that particular outfit as he prepared to create a new version for *The Cher Show*, the Broadway musical that looked back at the icon's life. 'She walks in like she's in her jeans. That's part of [her] charisma,' he said during an interview with *Entertainment Weekly*. And he's absolutely right. In fact, jeans are a great place to start when you're thinking about wearing something out there. Imagine a cropped jacket encrusted with beads. Pair it with tight leather trousers or a similarly embellished skirt and you're in danger of looking a bit like an extra on *The Cher Show*. A lo-fi vest top and high-waisted jeans that flare towards the hem, however, will dial down the showy element a notch.

Beads aren't as common an embellishment as sequins or studs, so it's worth browsing resale sites or digging through charity shops to find vintage pieces such as evening dresses, capes, belts and occasion bags embroidered with tiny spheres for added twinkle.

DON'T BE AFRAID TO EMBELLISH

CRYSTALS

At 2017's Billboard Music Awards, Cher performed two of her greatest hits – 'If I Could Turn Back Time' (1989) and 'Believe' (1998) – as she was honoured with the Icon Award. (Subsequent recipients have included Celine Dion, Janet Jackson and Mary J. Blige.) Cher being Cher, she did a nifty outfit change between the bangers, emerging in an ice-blonde wig with a hot pink hem for a rousingly camp version of 'Believe'. It was her outfit that stole the show, however. Crystallised ropes garlanded her shoulders, dripped from her waist and outlined her breasts, one of which was covered with a heart-shaped nipple pasty that was similarly tickled pink. It was a knock-out, a testament to the fact that a little sparkle goes a long way (and a lot of sparkle goes even further).

For an everyday approach, try a crystal tennis necklace or bracelet, which definitely shouldn't be saved for best. Like studs, crystals have also entered the mainstream when it comes to embellished footwear (again, you can thank ALAÏA). Think of them as a playful finishing touch to any outfit that's otherwise a bit, well, boring: a trouser suit, say. Crystals will give it oomph and then some.

PEARLS

With their traditional partner being a twin-set, pearls aren't the kind of embellishment that springs to mind when you picture Cher. Of course, you'd be wrong. She wears them in a way that never recalls politicians, royals or the aristocracy, but instead projects a mood that is much less 'establishment'. Attending a party in 2024, Cher paired jeans with a corset that had rows of pearls embellishing its boned structure, as well as twinkling crystals. The combination of pearls and crystals was pared back ever so slightly by the proximity of denim. It was a masterclass in how to modernise pearls, although you don't have to wear a corset to achieve a similar effect. A handful of contemporary jewellery brands are mixing pearls and crystals to make earrings which will immediately add a point of difference to, say, a white shirt. Almost anything can be given the pearly treatment, from wide-legged jeans whose surface has been dotted with tiny seed pearls, or a handbag with a clasp that's embellished by a single freshwater pearl, to a stiletto-heeled pump with a strap over the foot adorned with polished orbs. Follow Cher's example and wear them with something 'every day' – the aforementioned pumps with khaki cargo pants, or the jeans with a white T-shirt – to channel her lo-fi approach to pearls.

SHAKE UP YOUR

'When I'm home, I don't put on all that shit. When I'm *on camera* I want to look like I'm on camera – not like I'm sitting at home.'

CHER

Cher grew up in a house full of glamorous women, observing their rituals with the eyes of an impressionable kid who already knew she wanted a taste of fame. As she said on *The Jennifer Hudson Show*, 'There were three of them my mum [and her] two girlfriends, and they were all models and bit-part actresses. I would stand behind them and [...] watch them do their make-up and think, *Oh my God, these women are so amazing. I want to be this. I want to play with that.*' And play she would, using the sorcery of make-up she'd learned as a little girl to alternately draw in and dazzle her audiences, constantly reinventing the very idea of Cher.

Her album covers show the story of her make-up evolution. For *Chér* (1966), the singer's heart-shaped face takes up the entire cover, with the whole photograph rendered dreamily soft focus by the dry ice that presumably was pumped into the studio as she posed, chin resting in her palms. The most arresting thing about the portrait is her eyes, which are expertly framed with two ellipses of black liner which meet in the inner corner and extend in a gentle flick at the outer. It was her make-up signature throughout the sixties – a heavily lined eye which sometimes featured a frosted lid and peeked out from underneath the fringe covering her eyebrows – with lips that were relatively unadorned by comparison. What came later was a much bolder approach, with multi-coloured eyelids or dramatically shaded cheekbones. On the cover of *Stars* (1975), Cher's look reflects the intoxicating glamour of a newer, sexier decade, with a wet-look cherry lip, long feathered lashes and purple shadow smudged towards a perfectly arched brow.

It can't have been a coincidence that 1975 was also the first year of her TV show *Cher*, for which she commanded her very own dream team of hair stylist (Jim Oertel), make-up artist (Ben Nye II), wig-maker (Renate Leuschner) and manicurist (Minnie Smith), all of whom helped to enhance her shimmering get-ups made by Mackie. 'Enhance' is an understatement. Hair and make-up were vital in the creation of this particular Cher.

On episode 25, on which David Bowie appeared as a guest, one of her outfits was a plunging black gown which flowed around her body like an inky liquid with a fringed black wig which was shorn by her ears. Her nails, meanwhile, were painted blood red, matching the set behind her – perhaps by accident but more likely by very careful design. Another outfit, which she wore to groove next to the rock star as they sang a medley which included Bowie's 'Young Americans' (1975), was a caped white blouse styled with a triangular wig the colour of a tangerine, matching the tint of her guest star's slicked-back crop within a shade or two. In both cases, it was the accompaniments that made the clothes, elevating them from a gown to a 'look', something calculated to keep people tuning in, week after week. Sometimes

SHAKE UP YOUR MAKE-UP

outrageous but always mesmerising, Cher's make-up is as much a part of her mythology as her clothes and her voice. This is how to capture its magic for your own routine.

REMEMBER, MAKE-UP

Cher certainly utilised all the tools in her arsenal when it came to make-up, sculpting each cheekbone and lengthening every lash for the benefit of whichever camera's lens she was facing, but she also knew it was make believe, a form of wizardry which didn't have much to do with real life. In 1982, she agreed to a sit-down with Andy Warhol's *Interview* magazine, speaking with the artist as well as editor-in-chief Bob Colacello. Cher hinted that, as a star, it was a rare luxury to be able to go bare-faced because of the public's expectations, but also because of her own, which had been shaped by growing up without much in the way of frivolity, referencing a childhood spent moving around and without a father, who was in and out of prison. 'I've always been so wrapped up in material things because I was so poor when I was little. And now I stopped wearing make-up to go out. And I know that I really like to wear make-up, too, but I also want to be able to not have to,' she said.

SHAKE UP YOUR MAKE-UP

IS MAKE BELIEVE

As game-changing as it can be to apply your face to quite literally face the day, it's also important to remember, especially as we embark on a guided tour of Cher's sometimes fantastical hairstyles, that it can be just as empowering to wear no make-up at all. Cher did both, perhaps wishing that she'd be able to do more of the latter, as she says opposite. The best-case scenario is to find a middle ground so that you always feel like your best self, whether you're contoured to perfection or freshly moisturised but otherwise make-up free. This is something that comes with time but also a willingness to experiment, occasionally getting it wrong but always having fun.

SHAKE UP YOUR MAKE-UP

LIPS

Outside films, Cher doesn't often play characters other than 'Cher'. But for the cover of *It's a Man's World* (1995), she became Eve-like, with a fine arch of pencilled eyebrow and a blood-red lip, as well as a serpent curling around her body. You might want to resist the siren call of tweezers for obvious reasons, but you can definitely have fun with a dark shade of lipstick like carmine, applying a matte layer before a slick of gloss for shine.

EYES

Cher likes larger-than-life eye make-up, often applying metallic pigments from lash to brow. At 1983's Academy Awards, she went a step further, wearing a combination of pink and turquoise in alternating blocks of colour. For the cover of *Stars*, meanwhile, her lashes were teased up and out, curling towards the heavens for an effect that was eye-opening to say the least. For first-timers, I would recommend starting with one punchy shade before mixing in a second (Cher loves purple, wearing every hue on the spectrum from lilac to violet). You can also buy packs of individual false lashes – slightly less intimidating than a full set when it comes to application – which you can use to enhance your existing lashes so that they're volumised to the max (and positively Cheresque).

HAIR

Think 'Cher' and you also think of another four-letter word: 'hair'. Because whether it was left to flow down her back, a blanket of black that almost brushed the horse between her thighs on the cover of *Half Breed* (1973), or teased into a halo of curls for her role in *Mermaids* (1990), her hair is at least as attention-grabbing as what she's wearing, not so much an after-thought as meticulously planned to create a commotion.

On her variety show, Cher's costume changes – sometimes as many as 15 per episode – were accompanied by an increasingly elaborate array of hairstyles, only possible during the tight filming schedule thanks to the wardrobe of wigs maintained by Renate Leuschner. But the wigs weren't only a time-saver. They allowed her to shape-shift in front of the audience, a feat that continued long after her show was unceremoniously cancelled in 1976. Blonde, red, black, short, long and extra-long (her signature), Cher's done it all over her six decades in the spotlight.

Don't forget that just because you don't have a prime-time slot or a red-carpet appointment in your near future, it doesn't mean you can't take risks in the hair department. Perhaps you already wear wigs or have at least experimented with a clip-in fringe to miraculously change your look in under two seconds. Or maybe you're just looking for a style change to edge you a little out of your comfort zone. If that's the case, this guide will provide a wealth of inspiration from the woman herself...

1965

When she burst onto the scene in the sixties, Cher's hair reflected the decade's trend for a fringe so full and so straight as to cover the entire forehead with a shiny curtain. While it suited her bell-bottomed wardrobe – and was a look she occasionally reprised via a wig in later years – it was ultimately left behind, having served her faithfully until 1968.

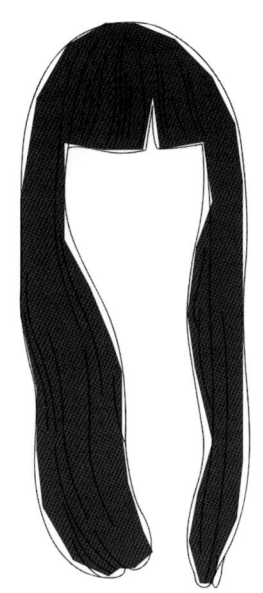

1971

In the early seventies, Cher's hair was often simply parted down the centre and left to fall in a sheet of black silk to well past her waist.

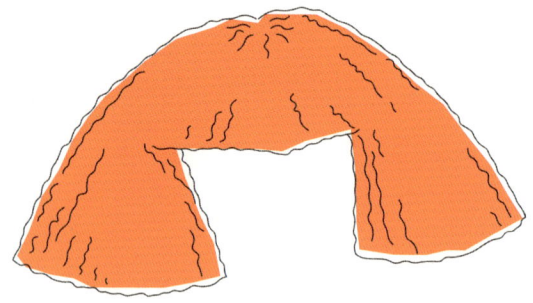

1975

When Bowie appeared on *Cher*, Cher wore an array of wigs, choosing a triangular style the colour of orange peel for their final, awe-inspiring medley.

Cher's hair was styled into an electrified mullet for a film première in 1985. She paired it with a flushed pink eyelid to reflect the decade's full-throttle approach to glamour.

1992

Performing in Las Vegas, the star dialled up the showgirl drama with a mane of curls whose softness contrasted with her sculpted lace bustier.

2000

Ever the showman, Cher switched the colour of her hair halfway through 2000's Emmy Awards, reappearing in the press room after the red carpet wearing an ice-blonde wig which mirrored her signature hip-length style of the seventies.

NAILS

Nails are part of the package, quite literally an extension of every fabulous outfit. And just like her hair, Cher's command attention. Her manicurist in the sixties and seventies was Minnie Smith, the nail veteran who administered to pop stars (Cher) and politician's wives (Nancy Reagan). In Smith's capable hands, Cher set a whole new trend when it came to shape, a squared-off end that was distinctive and daring instead of politely curved or pointed.

Cher is still wearing nails with her signature tip, as noticeably blunt now as they were in the early seventies, although perhaps a centimetre or two shorter and fractionally less pearlescent. You can easily shape yours at home with a file and a steady hand if you have strong nails that grow to a decent length.

If they're prone to breaking, however, why not experiment with press-ons, which you can apply with a special glue, or treat yourself to a set of false nails applied by a technician? Just don't hold back when it comes to colour. On the cover of February 1976's *Dynamite*, a children's magazine which came with a poster and that you can still buy on eBay, Cher's hands are wrapped around her body and resting on her shoulders, her nails painted the same lilac as her beaded (and backless) gown, but with metallic tips so they look as if they've been dipped in silver. If that didn't inspire the next generation to pay special attention to their nails, nothing could.

FIND THE

URS

THAT MAKE YOU FEEL FABULOUS

Terry Wogan: 'If you see a dress you like but you can't decide what colour you'd like it in, you buy all the colours?' Cher: '[...] I'm getting a little bit better. I buy three colours now instead of five.'

Cher has lived a more colourful life than most, especially when it comes to her wardrobe. Ever since she arrived on the scene in the sixties, she's gravitated towards shades that don't hold back (and combinations that are as playful as they are punchy). Think paisley-print bell bottoms in swirling pinks and greens. Or a vinyl mini dress in sunflower yellow with silver zippers. As she climbed the greasy pole of show business with Sonny, surely the point of such exuberant colours was to get noticed?

Her variety-show years signified a more glamorous approach to wearing colour. Gone was anything garish or girlish, to be replaced by a lustrous spectrum (courtesy of Mackie) which dazzled under the set lights – cerise, aquamarine and citrine, jewel-toned colours that signified a star was born.

By 1978, Cher had laid three shows to rest: *The Sonny & Cher Comedy Hour*, *Cher* and *The Sonny & Cher Show* (the ex-couple's second bite of the cherry as a double act, which was ultimately doomed). She emerged from her time on TV with a burning desire to make the leap to film, to be the 'serious actress' no one thought she could be. She didn't stop dressing with a devotion to razzmatazz, however. In fact, she turned the volume *up*. In a photo session the same year, wearing a wardrobe designed by Mackie, Cher's outfits were brief and the colours were bold, a visual sucker-punch which would have done little to quell the doubt about her suitability for cinema audiences.

One look was a turquoise bodysuit sewn with crystals. With her eyes closed and arms extended to the heavens, it made her look like a starfish in Spandex. But it was the so-called flame dress that really set pulses racing. The dress was a signature of Mackie's, who had already made a version for Tina Turner (a personal request after she spotted its sizzling hot tendrils of sequins on Raquel Welch). Cher, of course, made it her own, dancing in the shot with her arms outstretched as 'flames' of fire – red, orange and gold licked her lithe body, smouldering up her hips and down her sternum. A knock-out in every sense of the word, it was a testament to her desire to wear colour (or whatever took her fancy) rather than toning it down for Hollywood.

When she not only made it onto cinema screens but also won the industry's most prestigious award at the Oscars, Cher wore another strategically beaded gown, but this time in black. And that is the colour most associated with her wardrobe in the eighties – and, arguably, ever since, including the infamous leotard that would appear two years later in the music video for 'If I Could Turn Back Time'.

Whatever colour she's wearing, Cher always puts her unique stamp on the shade, making it entirely her own. In her hands, black can make a statement, while a razzle-dazzle silver can look suitable for every day – that's the genius of Cher.

CHER'S COLOUR CHART

1965–1971

SONNY & CHER

With colours that popped being all the rage in the sixties, Cher's wardrobe leaned in to a primary-coloured state of mind, with saturated red, blue and yellow. It was bold and a little brash, a girl's take on how to get attention.

FIND THE COLOURS THAT MAKE YOU FEEL FABULOUS

1971–1976

PRIME-TIME QUEEN

As Cher reigned at CBS, her wardrobe took on a jewel-toned appearance, with rich and lustrous hues to suit the slinky gowns and showgirl get-ups designed by Mackie.

TAKE ME HOME

Cher's gladiator-style armour went for gold on the album cover of *Take Me Home*.

1979

1983–1988

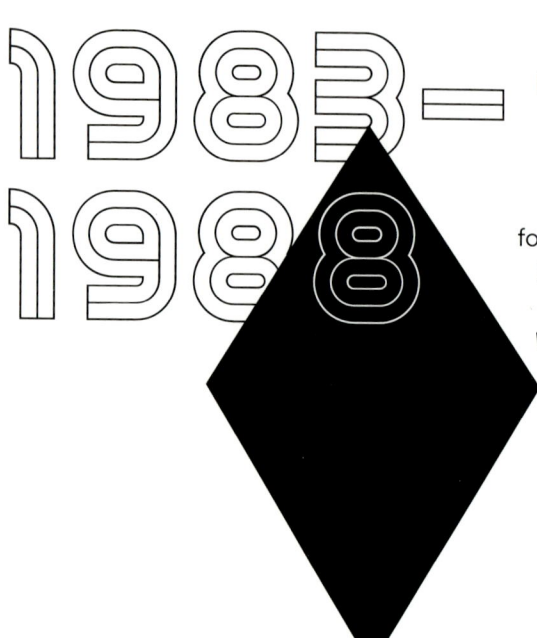

HOLLYWOOD COMES KNOCKING

Black was the colour that dominated her wardrobe for much of the eighties, from her award-season gowns to her costumes in *Mask*, *Witches of Eastwick* (1987) and *Moonstruck*.

LOVE HURTS

Cher's heart-shaped face took up the entire frame of the shot on the cover of *Love Hurts* (1991), her third album to ever go platinum. Her hair, however, wasn't blonde. Instead, she chose a burnished orange-red wig which she wore on and off throughout the nineties.

LIVING PROOF: THE FAREWELL TOUR

Cher was back with a bang for her Living Proof: The Farewell Tour, which most definitely wasn't a farewell to the kind of outfits that had made her a household name in the seventies. Starting out with a dramatic hooded coat, Cher's outfits shape-shifted in front of the audience until she wore nothing more than a crystal bra top with batwing sleeves.

CHER: HER STYLE PRINCIPLES

HOW TO WEAR
HEAD-
TO-
TOE

BLACK

In 1985, Cher appeared on *The Phil Donahue Show*. The format involved the host roving around the audience, asking them to pose questions to whomever was in the hot seat. Cher was promoting *Mask*, the film based on the true story of a boy who suffered from craniodiaphyseal dysplasia, and appeared wearing head-to-toe black, apart from a shock of ice blonde at the crown of a shorter, edgier crop. Her wardrobe and appearance were immediately a talking point. One woman asked, 'Are you glad you shed the glamorous, Barbie-doll image?' Cher replied, 'You mean I'm not glamorous?!' She was absolutely right to be faux-outraged, wearing a leather jacket, sheer tights, slender-heeled pumps and giant crystal earrings, each with a centre of heart-shaped black stone. It was just one example of how top-to-toe black became something of a wardrobe signature for Cher, who managed to make it look a little bit mind-blowing.

In *Mask*, Cher plays Rusty Dennis, a biker, single mother and badass who pulls no punches as she champions the interests of her son, Rocky. And her costumes, while

CHER: HER STYLE PRINCIPLES

relatively pared back and 'real', were also largely black, with the kind of leather mini skirts, strappy tops, scrunched boots, cord necklaces and biker jackets suited to jumping on the back of a motorcycle. Decades later, this is an excellent starting point when it comes to wearing black – and lots of it.

The next place you should look to for mood-board inspiration is the music video for 'If I Could Turn Back Time', where the concept of top-to-toe black remains but the glamour quota has increased by the power of ten (at least). Cher captained her own battleship for the occasion, the USS *Missouri*, with a bevy of sailors and a wardrobe that proved one thing: she might have an Oscar, but she still knew how to have fun. And fun, in this case, meant a sheer leotard which was essentially a plunging 'V': two strips of black material covering all her vital assets, with a thong at the reverse, suspenders and a silver belt that jangled in time as she danced on deck. The United States Navy was utterly scandalised – and so was MTV, who initially refused to air the video, eventually relenting but only for audiences post 9pm.

A bodystocking might be a no-go, but there are still takeaways when it comes to wearing black that will serve you in everyday life. Firstly, consider the mix of textures. Black might be preternaturally chic but it can look flat without any variation in material. For 'If I Could Turn Back Time', Cher mixed a shiny leather with sheer breaking up the colour black in a way that's just as dynamic today as it was then. (In fact, the leather was a last-minute addition. According to Mackie, who was interviewed by *Variety*, Cher was experiencing an emotion that wasn't very 'Cher': nerves. 'I call it the seatbelt outfit. She got so nervous with the sailors there, she put on her leather motorcycle jacket, and you [couldn't] see anything except this little strap that made that look worse. She loved it at the time, but it made her very nervous – and it's the only time I know she ever got that nervous.') On *The Phil Donahue Show*, it was the earrings (and perhaps the shock of platinum) that made her outfit pop.

Start with a basic like black trousers or a black knitted dress, then layer it with something in a different material, like chiffon, velvet, leather, corduroy or even denim. Make your finishing touch a statement accessory like a chain-link belt which slinks around the hips or crystal-and-pearl earrings that graze the shoulder like Cher's. See? Black doesn't have to mean boring.

HAVE A MOMENT

Cher often wore a single colour top to toe – and she didn't stop at black. In 1974, she performed as part of the Ringling Brothers Circus, standing on the big top's stage in a fire-engine red outfit of a sequined crop top, flares, cuffs and, of course, a top hat. On her TV show *Cher*, she wore a lot of white but made it anything but angelic, rewriting the colour's history via a criss-cross bra top with low-slung trousers which left a stretch of tummy on show. For her scene-stealing turn in *Mamma Mia! Here We Go Again!* (2018) – for which she reunited with her dear friend and former co-star Meryl Streep – she also wore top-to-toe white: a trouser suit which was as icily polished as her peroxide hair.

A monochrome outfit can be a powerful thing, hence why so many celebrities wear one colour on the red carpet, coordinating their clothes, shoes and even make-up to pack one hell of a punch in front of photographers. It can seem out there for this very reason, especially if you choose a primary colour or a jewel tone that comes with its own disclaimer: 'look at me'. But it's possible to make a subtle kind of statement with deeper shades (crimson and chocolate) or neutrals that create a sumptuous colour story when paired together (cream and butter).

FIND THE COLOURS THAT MAKE YOU FEEL FABULOUS

IN MONOCHROME

You also don't have to go for an entirely immersive effect. Another celebrity trick is to wear top-to-toe red but for the shoes, finishing the look with a gold pointed-toe pump, for example. Or a vest top and silky trousers, both in black, with a cord pendant necklace of red jasper. Remember: a block colour with a dash of something different can be just as impactful.

SEND A MESSAGE IN METALLICS

Cher and metallics go way back. She often wore them in a way that played up their unstoppable glamour. During a Beatles homage in an episode of *Cher*, with musicians wearing the candy-coloured uniforms of Sgt Pepper's Lonely Hearts Club Band, Cher wore a fringed silver bikini top which criss-crossed her bare stomach to a skirt of silver filaments. She was accompanied by two iconic guest stars, Tina Turner and Kate Smith. Despite a busy set that included a walk-on by a yellow submarine, you couldn't help but be captivated by the trio at the centre. If that outfit didn't make every woman at home want to ditch their housecoat and slippers for something slinky, sexy and silver, nothing could.

Cher also wore metallics to look almost understated. At a film première in 2001, she side-stepped a gown for an outfit that was altogether cooler: a gold frock coat sewn with crystals and metallised silver trousers. Paired with a white tank and square-toed boots, the result was rock-star effortless – and could easily be recreated by mixing two metallics, a flex considered a no-no by some but not by Cher. Ease yourself in by letting one colour lead, styling, say, a silver leather skirt with a chunky gold necklace or a gold brocade jacket with silver hoop earrings. Keep reading for outfit combinations that play gold against silver.

WHITE T-SHIRT
+
SILVER LEATHER SKIRT
+
CHUNKY GOLD
NECKLACE

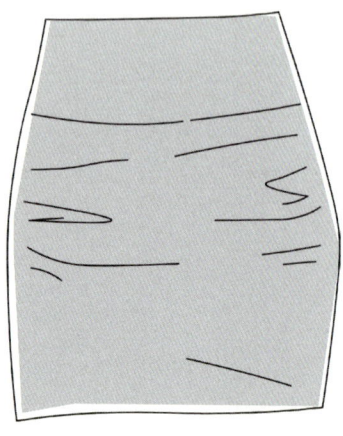

**GOLD BROCADE
JACKET**
+
WIDE-LEGGED JEANS
+
SILVER HOOP EARRINGS

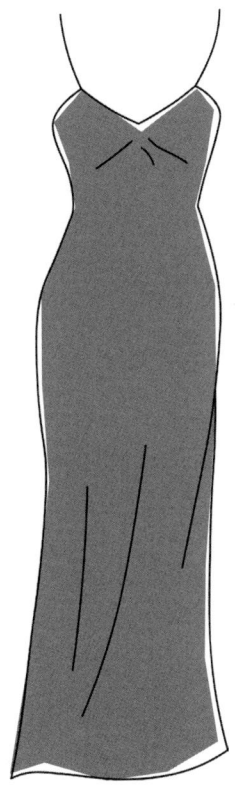

GUNMETAL SLIP DRESS

GOLD BANGLES

SUEDE KNEE-HIGH BOOTS

BLACK COLUMN DRESS

SILVER-STUDDED BELT

GOLD BALLET PUMPS

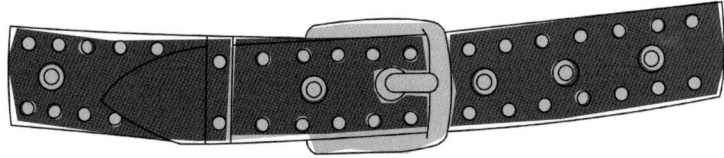

SAY 'YES' TO SURPRISING JEWEL TONES

Despite their lustrous shades, or perhaps because of them, jewel tones often get a bad rap for looking a little 'done', a little too *Dynasty*. When I think emerald, my brain thinks of the Academy Awards, conjuring exactly the kind of gown that would have kept the ceremony's overseers satisfied: a big swathe of satin which concealed rather than revealed. Cher, however, favours slightly more unusual jewel tones, shades that could be just as surprising as they were sumptuous to behold.

On one episode of *Cher*, she wore citrine, a luminous yellow much less obvious than gold, and amethyst, giving the purple shade more than a hint of spice with a bra top made of sequined peacock tail feathers. Other shades to consider include aquamarine, an icy blue; moonstone, an iridescent grey-white; and peridot, a glimmering yellow-green. A sequinned jewel-toned skirt would look fabulous with the simplest of garments: a mohair cardigan in a lighter shade of the same colour, for example, or a black long-sleeved jersey top which clings in all the right places. Semi-precious but playful, that's the name of the game.

LOVE YOUR

ROCK 'N' ROLL LEATHER

'I'm going to die wearing the same things that I love wearing. [...] I'm going to wear my leather jacket. I don't care. As long as I can look good in it, and feel comfortable in it, then I'm going to do it.'

CHER

CHER: HER STYLE PRINCIPLES

I n the music video for 'I Found Someone' (1987), Cher wore an outfit so era-defining, so iconic, that it was resurrected for fitness videos and 2017's Billboard Awards. It was a black peekaboo bodystocking, slashed here and sheer there, with a leather jacket. The video stars her real-life boyfriend at the time, Rob Camilletti, who became a never-ending source of intrigue for the gossip pages because of the job he was doing when he first crossed paths with Cher. He wasn't a gigging musician or a record executive but a man who made bagels for a living. 'I Found Someone' tells the story of an on-again, off-again couple whose relationship is played out on a dance floor. But despite featuring a truly spectacular outfit in the form of chainmail suspenders to match an armour-like mini dress, it's the cutaways between the club scenes that are the most rock 'n' roll: Cher singing on a moody blue-lit stage in the crystal-sewn bodystocking, with a leather jacket that slips, ever so coolly, off her shoulder as she performs.

The music video almost didn't get made. Geffen Records disagreed with her choice of co-star, refusing to let her cast Camilletti. Cher's response was to fund the video herself. If that isn't rock 'n' roll, what is? And she couldn't have done it wearing anything other than a leather jacket. Nothing semaphores a sense of effortlessness, or an utter disregard for the rules, better than leather. Which is probably why it became so associated with Cher.

She also played up the material's sex appeal to great effect. On the Love Hurts Tour (1992), Cher reprised a leather-look outfit from her eighties wardrobe. It was eye-poppingly ahead of its time – a bodysuit that gave more than a nod to kink with its rivets, chains and high-cut crotch, creating the most extraordinary silhouette (and leaving nothing to the imagination).

As someone who has always refused to play it safe, or dress in a way others find 'appropriate', Cher looked to leather as a go-to of sorts, just as much today as she did then. She wears it when she wants to go a little more incognito, but also when she wants to go all-out. For 2022's CFDA Awards, Cher chose a leather gown by Chrome Hearts, the top half of which was a deconstructed biker jacket, split open to hug the shoulders. (Incidentally, at the same event in 1993, where she posed backstage with legends such as Karl Lagerfeld, Cher also wore leather, this time a sleek pair of trousers with a giant crystal buckle at the waistband.)

Leather might be the coolest of the too-cool-for-school fabrics. In Cher's hands, however, it's more than cool. Sometimes tough, always sexy, this is how to do rock 'n' roll leather like the mistress of 'I don't give a damn'.

FINDING 'THE ONE'

Although she's worn many in her time, Cher usually gravitates towards a particular kind of leather jacket. Not a sleek blouson with a zip up the centre. Not a minimal blazer with a no-muss, no-fuss kind of mood. But a biker jacket which looks as if it's been around the block and earned its keep, slightly oversized, covered in zippers or studs – the definition of rock 'n' roll. The best place to find such a jacket is by combing the racks at your nearest vintage emporium, where there will undoubtedly be a whole range of leathers. As well as looking out for any defects – although those might contribute to the devil-may-care appeal of your new companion, FYI – seek out a style that comes up a little big so that its shoulders are slightly larger than yours and its sleeves reach at least past your knuckles; that way, you can hug it around your body or let it sexily drape off your arm.

THE ANATOMY OF A PERFECT LEATHER JACKET

(ACCORDING TO CHER)

LOVE YOUR ROCK 'N' ROLL LEATHER

Studs at the shoulders and sleeves

Oversized fit that's loose and louche

Extra zips for double the edge

Belt at the hemline (always left undone)

Cuffs that cover the wrist but preferably also the knuckles

CHER: HER STYLE PRINCIPLES

HOW TO GIVE YOUR LEATHER 'LOOK-TWICE' ENERGY

At 1997's Met Gala, which honoured the late fashion designer Gianni Versace, Cher was dressed by the fashion house in a body-hugging leather gown embellished with a twinkling crucifix on its left hip. And to this day, whenever she crosses paths with the brand Versace (Gianni's sister, Donatella, is a long-time friend), Cher's usually in some kind of leather creation that makes you want to look twice. For the brand's autumn/winter 2023 show in California, she appeared wearing an outfit that riffed on her look in the video for 'I Found Someone', a blue-black leather jacket which glittered with studs as she posed on the step-and-repeat, which she shrugged over a catsuit and paired with statuesque platform boots.

A leather gown is certainly head-turning but it's not exactly suitable for running errands (or even an after-dusk drink, unless the dress code is 'Met Gala'). You can still pump your leather with plenty of look-twice energy, however, simply by styling it with something that doesn't hold back, something that demands to be noticed. Why not play up an oversized biker jacket which skims the tops of your thighs with a slinky mini dress made of mesh? Or high-waisted black leggings tucked into thigh-high silver boots? You could also wear nothing underneath apart from a black lace bodysuit or bra, contrasting the lack of material up top with a witchy black skirt which skims the ankle and slits up one calf. Or flip the equation with a barely-there tank dress paired with fishnet tights and buckled biker boots, adding a statement accessory – say a chainmail earring or shoulder bag made of mirrored paillettes – to give the whole look a nudge towards glamour instead of grunge.

It's also worth looking for leather pieces that have look-at-me embellishments already. For a wickedly fun appearance on *Chicken Shop Date*, a quick-fire interview show filmed over nuggets and hosted by comedian Amelia Dimoldenberg, Cher wore a very special jacket made of brown, cream and black leather, with turquoise stones decorating the shoulders. Paired with a wavy sapphire wig, it was a lesson in giving your leather the right attitude: in this case, one that's all about standing out and owning your sex appeal. Try it.

DOUBLE DOWN ON DARING

DENIM

'My relationship with denim started when I was six years old. And it has gone on ever since. It is the longest relationship I have ever had.'

CHER

In 2000, Cher stole the show in a very special episode of *Will & Grace*, the smash-hit sitcom about a couple of best friends living in New York City. Jack McFarland, one of the titular duo's outrageous sidekicks, was obsessed with Cher – so obsessed that in this particular scene, he's in a restaurant accompanied by a doll of his idol, dressed in a spangled get-up which looks suspiciously like an original Mackie. His friends call him a 'freak' and leave. Then who should sweep over but the life-sized version of the woman whose plastic form has been placed, lovingly, on a booster seat: Cher. She's dressed in an outfit comprising all kinds of signatures, including a pair of flared jeans whose hems have been accentuated by trumpets of a tulle-like fabric. Not realising it's actually Cher, Jack proceeds to engage her in a conversation which culminates in a sing-off of 'If I Could Turn Back Time'. After Jack corrects her intonation, Cher slaps him, delivering her famous line from *Moonstruck* – 'Snap out of it!' – as a parting shot. Jack faints, but, really, he should have known better. Who could pull off those jeans but Cher?

Despite being best known for her showgirl get-ups, Cher's relationship with denim has been one of her most enduring; it's a key part of her wardrobe then and now. When she was interviewed on *The Dick Cavett Show*, Cher gave the host a descriptive tour of her tattoos, insisting that she wouldn't recommend them to anyone. Cavett took his opportunity, asking: 'What do you recommend?'. Cher quipped, 'I don't recommend anything. I recommend Levi's jeans. That's about the only thing.' While her taste in jeans might have shifted through the decades – flared in the seventies, bleached in the eighties, straight in the nineties and baggy in the noughties – the way she wears her true blues hasn't changed all that much. She serves them up with something unexpected – a pearl-embellished corset, say – or plays with the surface of the denim itself, whether that's with a constellation of iridescent rhinestones or an eclectic mix of patches to remedy wear and tear.

Having said that, Cher is nothing if not surprising. On the opening night of Studio 54, on 26 April 1977, she was helped down the club's infamous steps by its co-owner Steve Rubell. This wasn't because she'd arrived in her usual finery, with a perilous satin train that could have sent anyone tumbling, but rather because of her footwear: statuesque mule sandals. Her clothes, in fact, were distinctly pared back considering this was the opening of the year or even decade – a simple combination of straight-legged jeans and a sweater that nonetheless looked fabulous, a lo-fi approach to glamour that suited her just as much as her all-singing, all-dancing costumes on TV. That pair of jeans spoke for itself, unadorned and still utterly captivating on Cher.

Dressed up or dressed down, she has always stayed true to denim. Here's how to sprinkle a bit of the same magic on the wardrobe staple you probably wear day in, day out.

CHER: HER STYLE PRINCIPLES

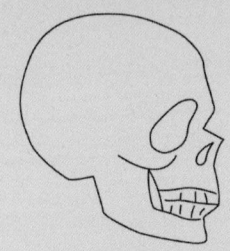

GIVE YOUR DENIM THE GLOW-UP IT DESERVES

Jeans might have been a uniform of sorts for Cher over the years, but they have been anything but a blank canvas. Instead, they have been bleached to create a tie-dye effect and patched with a pair of hearts on each thigh and rips at the knee. Or coated with a sparkle that could rival her costumes on *Cher*. Or interrupted by swathes of leather snaking down her legs.

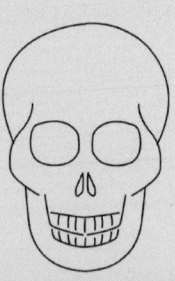

If a frayed knee or prominent whiskers constitutes 'wild' in your wardrobe of jeans, why not dig out an old pair that hasn't seen the light of day for a year or two and think about how you could give them a glow-up? Unless you're handy with a needle and thread (very handy), I wouldn't suggest attempting to patchwork or decorate anything yourself. Instead, seek out denim brands or high-street retailers that offer customisation services in their stores (or allow you to send off your jeans for embellishing with embroidery, patches or even paint). It's great for revitalising a pair that's been sitting in your wardrobe, either because you've fallen out of love with them or because they're in need of repair. Cher might choose an assortment of patches (stars, hearts and skulls are favourites), a constellation of strass crystals over the pockets, or a dip-dye effect to create a spectrum of blues.

With such a pair of jeans at your disposal, you can relax when it comes to what to wear on your top half. For a photo session in 1987, Cher sat on an extraordinary shag couch, the fuzzy surface of its seat cushions melding seamlessly with the sheepskin rug at her feet, wearing jeans that were bleached, patched, ripped and, essentially, fabulous with a capital 'F'. Letting the jeans speak for themselves, she wore a scoop-neck cotton top with its sleeves pushed up to her elbows, the ideal partner for something that demands to be noticed.

TAKE DOUBLE DENIM SERIOUSLY

Double denim used to be a kind of punchline, a trend from the (some might say) style desert of the early noughties, best left in the past along with low-rise waistbands and visible whale tails. Cher was rocking the combination at least a decade earlier, giving it more than a shade of glamour. A lot of people mix denims together, creating a patchwork effect that can work as a marginally less 'in your face' approach. In Cher's book, however, 'in your face' is no bad thing. She regularly wore a denim jacket colour-matched to her jeans, pairing it with a strappy camisole top embellished with a corsage. For another outing, she wore a stone-washed set with a beaded shoulder bag to pep up her true-blue uniform to perfection. Before you get to accessories, however, you could also play with the denim set in question. It doesn't have to be jeans and a jacket. A tailored waistcoat and a maxi skirt, for example, would make an excellent substitute, especially if styled with scrunched knee-high boots. A sculpted denim bustier with baggy jeans is another winning idea. And if anyone gives you grief about the fact you're wearing double denim, kindly direct them to Cher.

EMBRACE
AN

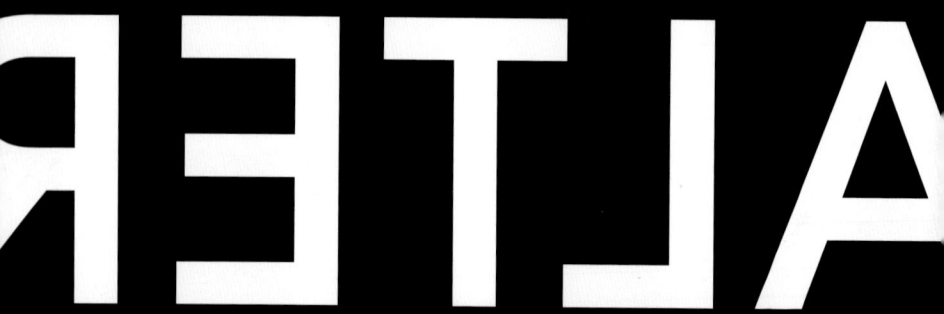

EGO

'I still want to look really attractive and I still like to get dressed up, but it's a terrible thing to know that you have to look a certain way for people to like you.'

CHER

Cher's alter-ego is her larger-than-life stage persona, bedazzled enough to outshine a supernova. This is the version presented to the public via her music videos, films and red-carpet premières (gleefully fuelled by the gossip columns who churned out titillating and mostly untrue stories week in, week out). One of the reasons she put on this regalia was to keep doing her job as an entertainer (and to live up to people's expectations). As she put it on *The Phil Donahue Show*, 'If I walked in here in jeans and a T-shirt, I think that would be a little disappointing for everybody.' But she also has an off-camera personality, her 'real' alter-ego: the person she is away from the bright lights and incessant camera lenses, with a style all of her own.

For a 2023 cover interview in *Paper* – the same magazine that 'broke the internet' with a deliciously salacious, semi-naked editorial of Kim Kardashian – Cher looked straight into the camera, eyes surrounded by clusters of gold crystals, hair whipped into an ice-blond beehive of towering proportions. Her gold-and-black bodysuit, almost reptilian and burnished by thousands of glimmering sequins like hyper-glamorous scales, was by Versace. During the interview itself, however, the writer only mentions one item of Cher's clothing: track pants. (It was a similar story decades earlier in 1982, for her famous interview with Andy Warhol, when the star greeted her guests in a lo-fi combination of 'black jogging pants' and 'white running shoes'.)

Cher, by most accounts (but also surprisingly), is always happiest in jeans and a T-shirt, face scrubbed clean of make-up. She has always been a woman of superb taste, as well as having the kind of charisma that makes clothes look international. And that applies to her off-duty wardrobe as much as the stage get-ups she's worn for her many, many tours.

She also loves to shop and is rarely left to browse in peace by the paparazzi, who followed her to Madison Avenue on what must have been a short reprieve from set in November 1975. Cher was captured looking nothing like Cher, wearing a plaid shirt with rolled cuffs and slim-fit cream trousers tucked into chestnut knee-high boots. Her only concession to 'glamour' was a pair of tinted sunglasses – brown to match the neutral colour palette of her outfit – shielding her eyes from the waiting flashbulbs. Somehow it was just as compelling as any album cover: a snapshot of her personal style that told a different story, and one that, crucially, had nothing in common with her day job.

The good news is that, unlike some of the regalia we've explored in this book, these down-to-earth yet decidedly chic looks can be copied without looking so obviously Cher. There's her side hustle as a late-seventies 'airport influencer', for example. Or the outfit formula she relied on for retail therapy sessions. And, finally, the movie roles that featured a grittier kind of realism, a far cry from the fantasy of sequined gowns held together with spirit glue. It's not just about emulating her wardrobe away from the spotlight. It's more about not being afraid to switch up your style and, most importantly, finding the confidence to defy people's expectations. After all, Cher does both, and so can you.

THE OG AIRPORT INFLUENCER

Most of us view the airport as a necessary evil to reach our destination. That's not the case for your average celebrity, however, who's come to see departures as their own personal runway. Nice Airport welcomes particularly stylish travellers every year for the Cannes Film Festival, where the so-called 'fits ranging from soft-power suiting to statement tracksuits have turned the act of touching down into a fashion 'moment' as valuable as the red carpet's step-and-repeat. But the original airport influencer was undisputedly Cher.

EMBRACE AN ALTER-EGO

In 1977, she flew into LAX, where the paparazzi lay in wait, poised to get a shot of the star with her former husband, Sonny Bono (the pair had been on the road as part of their short-lived reunion act after the cancellation of *Cher*). Side-stepping comfy separates and flat shoes for an outfit with infinitely more swagger, Cher looked statuesque in a pair of thigh-high snake-print boots. It was a relatively casual look otherwise – practical even – with indigo jeans, a tunic blouse, a low-slung belt and aviator sunglasses. But the stacked boots, towering and terrifically sexy, made for the kind of photograph that would be splashed on front covers.

Other travelling companions over the years have included a raffia cowboy hat (1974), leather trousers accessorised with a belt that jangled with chunky heart-shaped charms (1984) and a fringed velvet scarf draped around the collar of a black overcoat (1998). In each case, a statement accessory was used to head-turning effect. And while you might not have a phalanx of photographers waiting post-flight (thank goodness), why not put a little effort into what you're wearing the next time you're about to take off?

THE 'CASUAL' OUTFIT FORMULA

Here's the thing: Cher's version of casual is still pretty spectacular. In 1978, the singer lent her vocals to a telethon supporting United Cerebral Palsy, forgoing her usual glitz and glamour for the comparatively pared-back outfit of a checked shirt, black leggings and knee-high boots. Because it was Cher, however, the outfit was more than the sum of its parts, effortless but also enigmatically sexy, precisely because it concealed rather than revealed. As well as trying out a similar trifecta, balancing out the proportions of an oversized button-down with a sculpted pair of leggings and heeled knee-highs, you could use each component of that particular outfit separately, as they are versatile enough to be leveraged into multiple looks for all manner of occasions.

EMBRACE AN ALTER-EGO

CHECKED SHIRT

Denim jacket	Knitted slip dress	Leather jacket	Baggy jeans
+	+	+	+
Wide-legged chinos	Leather flip-flops	White maxi skirt	Suede ballet pumps
+	+	+	+
Leather loafers	Aviator sunglasses	Slouchy knee-high boots	Silver bangle

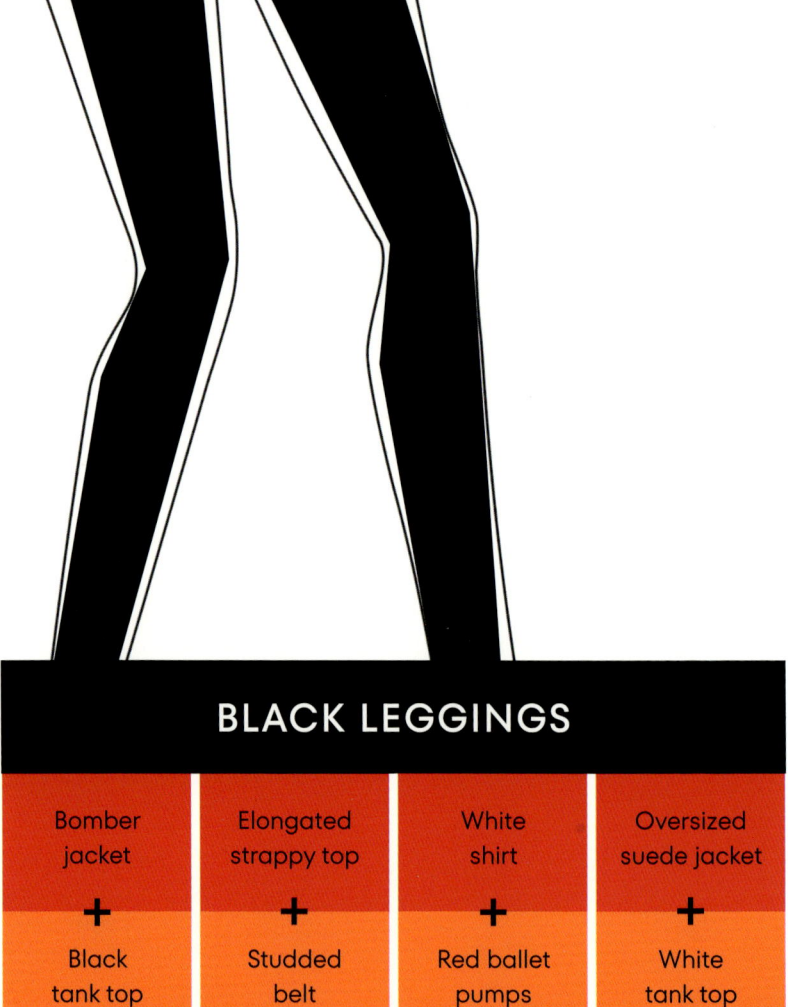

BLACK LEGGINGS

Bomber jacket	Elongated strappy top	White shirt	Oversized suede jacket
+	+	+	+
Black tank top	Studded belt	Red ballet pumps	White tank top
+	+	+	+
Mock-croc mini heels	Leather clogs	Silver hoop earrings	Black riding boots

EMBRACE AN ALTER-EGO

KNEE-HIGH BOOTS			
Sweater dress	Black polo neck	Crew-neck jumper	White shirt
+	+	+	+
Chunky belt	Denim midi skirt	Bermuda shorts	Slim-fit jeans

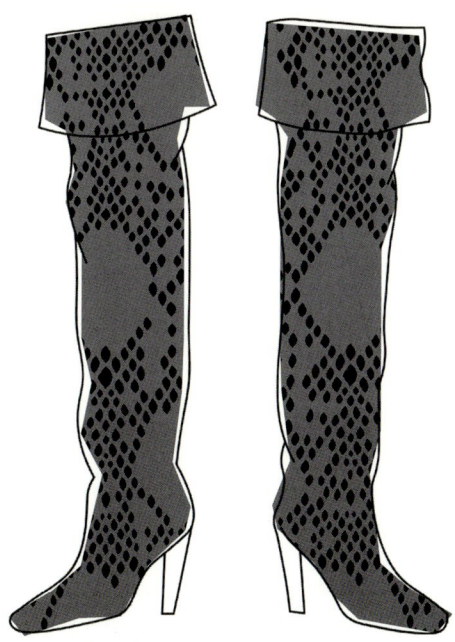

CHER: HER STYLE PRINCIPLES

HOLLYWOOD CALLS,

CHER ANSWERS...

In 1983, Cher finally got her break on the silver screen. Mike Nichols approached her about a part in *Silkwood*, the true story of a whistleblower at a nuclear facility which also starred Meryl Streep. The film followed Cher's successful run on stage in Broadway's *Come Back to the 5 & Dime, Jimmy Dean, Jimmy Dean*. Not only did the film capture the attention of the Academy Awards – Streep was nominated for Best Actress, Cher for Best Supporting Actress – but it also proved one thing definitively: against the odds, Cher was more than capable of playing a 'real' person. In *Silkwood*, she became Dolly Pelliker, a woman whose mullet hairstyle was often tied into twin pigtails and whose day-to-day uniform was a T-shirt, durable workman's trousers and cowboy boots. It couldn't have been more of a departure for Cher, who was usually poured into slinky, sexy or otherwise sizzling outfits courtesy of Mackie, but it constituted another reinvention, what you might call a 'make-under', which set her on the path to even greater stardom and critical acclaim. And when you think about fit, Pelliker's look wasn't all that different from that of off-duty Cher. (As she told journalist Philip Galanes, who interviewed her in 2018 for the *New York Times*, 'Listen, people have all kinds of ideas about me. There's the sparkly me and the quiet me. But the quiet me comes more naturally. If I could do *Silkwood* for the rest of my life, I'd be very happy.') To elevate an everyday look from a tee and jeans to something more, add a statement item such as tinted shades big enough to eclipse your eyebrows, or a vintage leather jacket. Having worn that combination many times, Cher would approve.

CHOOSE EYE-CATCHING ⭕ ⭕

ADD-

ONS

'Success is like different moments, like pearls, and if you string them on long enough you've got a necklace.'

CHER

At 1985's Met Gala, Cher was accompanied by her style partner-in-crime Mackie, who'd made her something typically stupendous to wear for her second time at the fashion world's equivalent of the Oscars. As he remembered during an interview with *Variety*: 'So, the skirt on this was simple and black. It's one layer of fine tulle and beads. The rest is her skin showing. Anywhere that is not black is her skin. There were also the ear cuffs, which people went wild for.' Ah yes, the cuffs, two winged protrusions designed to cover the ear lobes, leaving the shells exposed and enhancing the ears' natural shape like they were being engulfed in gold flames. Spectacular. And just one example of how accessories can often make or break an outfit. The key is to always consider them as part of the ensemble, not an afterthought. Mackie included the cuffs in his original sketch, along with the hairstyle he thought would suit that high neckline, leaving nothing to chance on the night.

CHOOSE EYE-CATCHING ADD-ONS

The one person who doesn't need advice about how to accessorise is Cher, whose 'more is more' mantra when it comes to getting dressed has always included a liberal approach to add-ons, such as a feathered black-and-purple headdress curling around her cheekbones and matching her eye make-up. Even when she's off stage and out of costume, she often gravitates towards adornment: a choker-style necklace covering the neck, throat and collarbone in twinkling ropes of black gemstones, for example. In most cases, it has been the accessory that elevates the outfit, not the other way round, making a statement that is distinctly Cher.

And if a feathered headdress or a multi-stranded choker sounds too much, how about starting with something a little more ordinary, like shoes? Having said that, Cher's taste in footwear isn't what you'd call modest. When she was filming *Cher*, Fred Slatten was personally making her shoes, as well as half of Hollywood's (the stylish half). The *Los Angeles Times* gave the headline of his obituary a rather telling addendum when he passed away in 2015: 'Fred Slatten dies at 92; king of crazy-high heels and platform shoes'. His Santa Monica Boulevard shop was the place to go – the only place – if you wanted to walk in the footsteps of the era's pop stars, rockers and beautiful people. Cher often needed the boost of a platform heel to elongate the already-sinuous lines of her satin gowns. So the next time you're debating between a flat and a heel – not perilously high but high nonetheless – remember, Cher wouldn't have considered it a choice at all.

Keep reading to learn how to make an accessory the star of the show that is your outfit, from a cluster of necklaces to the most statement-making boot of all time.

CHER: HER STYLE PRINCIPLES

LAYER YOUR NECKLACES

Cher played against type in *Tea with Mussolini* (1999), a delightful period drama co-starring three dames, Judi Dench, Maggie Smith and Joan Plowright, as well as Lily Tomlin, who'd previously appeared on *Cher*. Cher's character in the film, Elsa Morganthal Strauss-Armistan, was finger-curled, thinly browed and immaculately dressed in black and white, often costumed in nipped-waist ensembles, veiled hats and pearls, lots of pearls, entirely befitting of a rich and powerful woman in the forties. And while pearls have a habit of looking a little traditional, Cher gave them a hint of something more subversive in one scene by wearing them with a close-fitting sweater, looping multiple stands around its unzipped collar to up the ante. It's a styling trick that mirrors an earlier proclivity of Cher's – a multi-stranded pearl necklace she wore not around her neck but looped over her left shoulder and under her right arm so that it criss-crossed her body for a twist on a classic that was not just unexpected, but possibly never seen before or since. If you don't have a pearl necklace long enough to create a lasso effect, you can still layer yours with other necklaces to create a neckline that's cluttered in the best kind of way. Contrast longer strands with chokers that sit close to the throat, adding a pendant into the mix for a point of difference.

GO THIGH-HIGH

'Spandex and sex': in a video interview with *Vogue*, that's how Cher described a certain turquoise bodysuit that she wore as part of a photoshoot in 1978. But it was the boots she wore with that bodysuit that were actually from her own wardrobe, a thigh-high silver pair with cuffs that gave them a swaggering kind of energy. The good news is that you don't have to wear your thigh-high boots with anything resembling exercise gear, although they are the ideal plus-one for black high-waisted leggings. Instead, try slim-fit jeans smoothed into your boots, an oversized sweater and a coat that brushes just below the mid-calf. A jersey dress that stops at the upper thigh, allowing for a sliver of skin between its hemline and your over-the-knee boots, is also a very good idea. As for the boots themselves, they don't have to be metallic. Look for a pair that isn't designed to suction to your calf but instead allows you to scrunch the leather ever so slightly, so the height can be tweaked depending on the outfit.

CHER: HER STYLE PRINCIPLES

MAKE YOURS A MULE

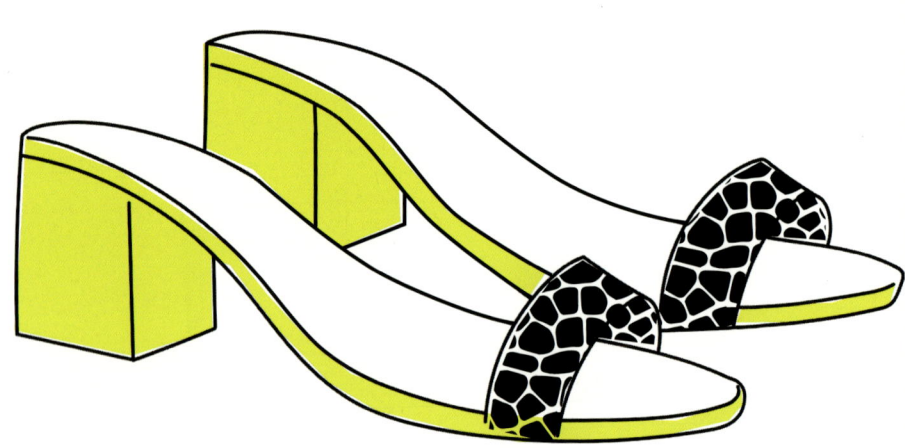

Cher might be known for performing in towering platform sandals but off stage she is just as taken with mules, a backless sandal or shoe with a strap across the upper foot which is coquettish and cool. As heels, they're not especially comfortable in all honesty, owing to the pressure that builds on the ball of your foot without much in the way of support. But what they lack in practicality, they make up for in looks. The mule is capable of turning the most 'basic' outfit into something worth beholding. Cher loves wearing hers with jeans, elevating the casual personality of denim into a much sexier proposition with a simple change of shoes. Look for styles with a height of no more than six centimetres; it's even better if the heel is a slender wedge or something more substantial than a pencil-thin stiletto. Make sure you choose something with 'big shoe energy', which could be delivered via a mock-croc leather, a crystallised upper or a mesh strap. And psst: wear them around the house before stepping outside to break them in as well as possible.

CHER: HER STYLE PRINCIPLES

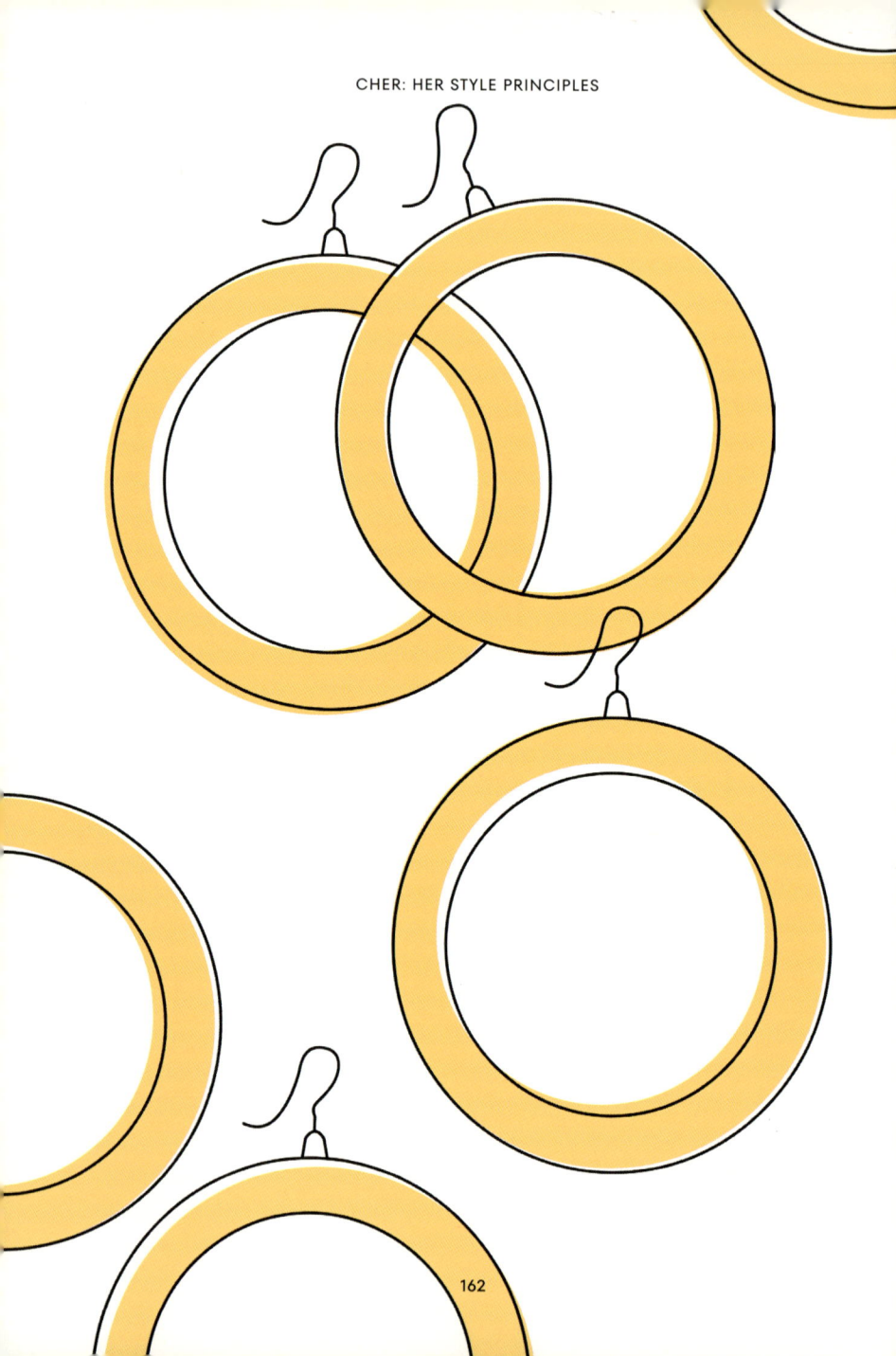

SAY SOMETHING WITH STATEMENT EARRINGS

Cher has become a front-row regular, lending a legend's star power to fashion shows including Balmain (where she actually graced the catwalk with the label's creative director, Olivier Rousteing), Versace and Valentino. And she's cultivated a uniform of sorts for these events, much like your average fashion editor who falls back on top-to-toe black, usually arriving in tailoring and wide-legged trousers with a final twist in the form of chandelier-style earrings grazing the collarbone. It's a bold look but not one she's recently discovered. No, Cher and earrings that err on the side of making a statement go way back. She's worn gold hoops with the circumference of a small orange and crystal-heavy clip-ons which drip with a pendant costume jewel at the centre. You're probably on first-name terms with hoops, whether you prefer a stack of pavé huggies or a single pair big enough to double as a bangle. Cher typically opts for the latter, often styling hers with a jersey bandeau top (the kind that became popular in the seventies and returned in the early noughties only to persist ever since), but they're the kind of plus-one that you can add to any outfit formula.

CHOOSE A CROWNING GLORY

When *Believe* was released in 1998, Cher was back where she belonged: at the top of the charts. Its title song became a universal anthem for anyone who's ever had their heart broken, while its use of Auto-Tune, a pitch-correction software, made it a phenomenon. It also signified a new style era for the pop goddess, who appeared in the music video wearing a metallised trouser suit in keeping with the decade's minimalist aesthetic. She couldn't resist a flourish, however: a headdress made from a fountain of tubular plastic lengths. This last-minute addition was made by a man who just happened to be on set while they were filming.

He'd been crafting – presumably, to pass the time – when who should walk by? Cher, who promptly commissioned a bigger version for the video.

Cher's worn hats since the very beginning. For off-camera moments when she was catching a flight or grabbing lunch between takes, it was usually a straw cowboy hat sourced from Charlie Tweddle, a legendary craftsman who made the cherry on top for musicians like Kris Kristofferson. On *Cher*, Mackie would sketch elaborate headdresses to go with certain outfits, from the now-controversial war bonnets paired with criss-cross crop tops, to a white cowboy hat with a feathered plume. When she appeared on *Carol Burnett: 90 Years of Laughter + Love* (2023), Cher recycled a favourite tour outfit, a gold beaded gown which was given a halo that burst with sunbeams. It was almost celestial – a fitting tribute to the godmother of variety TV, Burnett – and wouldn't have looked anywhere near as godly without its crown.

Most of us are either a hat person or not a hat person. Cher is most definitely the former, so why not experiment with a crowning glory that's all your own? A cowboy hat or halo might be pushing it but, really, the simplest topper can make a statement, especially if you're not used to wearing one. Consider baseball caps, beanies and wide-brimmed straw hats as your gateway. Once you've got used to the feeling, however, add buckets, berets and fedoras into the mix. The best news? It's a bad-hair day fix and a two-second trick for looking more like Cher.

DECIDING HOW MUCH IS TOO MUCH

CHOOSE EYE-CATCHING ADD-ONS

One of the most oft-repeated fashion 'rules' is that before you leave the house you should take one thing off, often an accessory, the last thing you threw on with little sense of ceremony. The received wisdom is that, by casting a critical eye over what you're wearing and removing whatever's surplus to requirements, you're left with an outfit that's sharper and, crucially, the opposite of trying too hard. Cher, however, often takes a different path, adding everything from earrings to necklaces to belts to bags, for not only double but quadruple the fun, proving that whoever coined the aforementioned rule was a little too concerned with so-called 'taste'.

Perhaps you're already someone who piles it on, adding points of interest to every outfit with a brooch on your lapel, a chain necklace hung with charms, a bangle stack or a handbag that itself has been accessorised. If so, carry on. For those of us who are more cautious, failing to commit to even one plus-one per outfit, it's time for a new chapter when it comes to accessorising. 'More is more' is now your modus operandi. So wear a pair of earrings *and* a necklace (Cher did it all the time, except she also added bracelets, several cocktail rings and a hairdo that was hair-raising into the equation, FYI). Adorn your wrists with childish abandon. Opt for a playful bag instead of something practical that can hold the kitchen sink.
In Cher's world, there's no such thing as too much.

EXPERIMENT WITH BIG-PERSONALITY

'I always dress strangely because I kind of think it's fun. And I think people enjoy seeing things on television that they can't see everywhere.'

CHER

CHER: HER STYLE PRINCIPLES

When it came to putting together a character list for *Cher*, her character Laverne was air-lifted over from *The Sonny & Cher Comedy Hour*. Laverne was Cher's only creation to be resurrected for her solo act on CBS. And for good reason: Laverne proved to be TV gold. Her USP, as well as the wad of gum permanently wedged in her cheek, snapping between zingy one-liners, was her costume, a tiger-print all-in-one with stirrups around the arch of each foot, stacked gold mules, an outrageous amount of baubles (cuffs, beaded necklaces and earrings), rhinestone-studded cat-eye glasses and, crucially, a bra strap that always fell down one shoulder, a stroke of genius by Mackie. Laverne's style was like her personality: loud and unapologetic, enhanced by the fact she would clash those big-cat stripes with a floral scarf tied around her coiffed orange curls. It might have been a costume, and a walking, talking advert for so-called 'bad' taste, but it wasn't totally out of character for Cher. Because like her wisecracking alter-ego who loves to gossip in the laundromat, Cher similarly gravitates towards the bold and the unabashed when it comes to print.

In the sixties, it was primary-coloured stripes on a pair of bell bottoms, whose punchy lines in red, blue and yellow elongated her legs until they were impossible to ignore. Or a checkerboard mini dress with alternating squares of green and white, which would have created a rather butter-wouldn't-melt effect if it weren't for her wickedly black eyeliner. In the eighties, she graduated to florals, whether they were blown up so that one flower head covered a hip, or worn as a denser pattern on a damask-like fabric. In the noughties, she once again walked on the wild side, bringing back animal print back in the form of leopard-spotted or tiger-striped coats, which made a different kind of statement from liquid-silk or sequined gowns on the red carpet.

Print can be intimidating if you feel comfortable in solid colours, but it can also add excitement or even intrigue to an outfit that's otherwise a little 'safe'. You don't have to go full Laverne, although tiger print is now a perennial on the catwalks, season in, season out. Just try introducing a splash of something – a polka dot or a zig-zag stripe – it might be just the shake up an outfit needs. For Cher's iconic turn at 1986's Oscars, her latticed crop top created a grid pattern on the skin of her throat and décolletage, a moment for the fashion history books and one that landed her on the front pages of newspapers around the world. Newsprint might not be your goal when it comes to, well, print, but it can't hurt to dream big.

THE PATTERN INDEX

STRIPES

Cher embraced the bell-bottomed silhouette with gusto, leaning in to the trousers' more-is-more personality with primary-coloured stripes.

CHECKERBOARD

Channelling the pop ingenues of the sixties, Cher's checkerboard mini dress in alternating squares of white and green was a girlish approach to print which suited her early hits.

FLORALS

Think of florals and you might not immediately think of Cher, whose style personality is the opposite of a wallflower. Luckily, she found a style of floral to suit her taste: a little moody (and a lot of glamour).

ANIMAL PRINT

Laverne stuck to her style guns with tiger print (or occasionally leopard) – and her creator is also partial to big-cat stripes or spots on the red carpet.

HEARTS

Unusually cutesy for Cher, this heart print appeared on *The Sonny & Cher Comedy Hour* (an ironic choice, perhaps, as it was the same year the show was cancelled because its co-hosts had parted ways). The print was created, however, out of sequined hearts. Now that is very Cher.

CHER: HER STYLE PRINCIPLES

ANIMAL ATTRACTION

EXPERIMENT WITH BIG-PERSONALITY PRINTS

Animal print's reputation for making a rather brash kind of statement has a long history, which owes much to small-screen icons such as Pat Butcher (*Eastenders*), Adriana La Cerva (*The Sopranos*) and, of course, Laverne, whose tiger-striped jumpsuit telegraphed her personality to perfection. (When Laverne leaves the laundromat in one episode for a very special visit to Liberace's, she's blown away by the chandelier in his foyer, not left speechless but instead quipping loudly, 'If they ever put my face on Mount Rushmore, that could be one of my earrings!' How much flatter would that one-liner have landed if she'd been wearing a bias-cut something or other? Exactly.) That was then. Whether you're wearing tiger, leopard or the lesser-spotted zebra now, animal print's personality has shifted these days, going from traffic-stopping or so-called 'bad' taste to something with a subtle kind of sex appeal, a neutral, even, which you can pull out any day of the week.

Aside from Laverne, Cher has been known to wear animal print to premières and parties as a more casual, but no less cool, take on red-carpet dressing. For a gala celebrating Aerosmith, the band chosen to be 2002's MTV Icon, Cher arrived in a suitably rock 'n' roll outfit: tight leather trousers, peroxide hair, smudged red eyeshadow and a tiger-print coat edged with turquoise stones. And in fact, animal-print outerwear is one of the easiest ways to project a bit of big-cat energy into your wardrobe. It doesn't have to be faux fur. A brushed wool coat with a slightly fuzzy texture will probably be more of a long-lasting investment, with leopard print being the perennial you'll see every season.

A pair of animal-print trousers is another path almost guaranteed to lead to a memorable outfit. It might feel a bit outrageous when you first stride out of the house but, trust me, style them with something classic like a navy cashmere jumper or a denim shirt over a white vest, and your bottom half will never feel the same in true-blue jeans again.

The final option is an animal-print plus-one, a well-chosen handbag or a pair of shoes to add a flourish of spots and stripes in a way that's subtly head-turning. Think ballet pumps, calf-hair loafers, a half-moon shoulder bag or even a belt to add a slice of something tantalising to the simplest of looks.

EXPERIMENT WITH BIG-PERSONALITY PRINTS

HOW TO PULL OFF A PRINT CLASH

For those who don't balk at the sight of a stripe or a spot, the next frontier – the ultimate flex, if you like – is clashing two patterns together. In one outfit. On the red carpet at 2021's opening gala for the Academy Museum of Motion Pictures, Cher arrived in not one print but two, wearing leopard-print flared trousers and a checkerboard bodice of black-and-cream panels. Offset with a hat similarly monochrome (and worn jauntily slanted), not to mention a lashing of chain and pearl necklaces, it might have been daring – certainly more so than a column gown or tuxedo – but it was also perfectly balanced with the addition of a blazer. Black with a border of cream piping, Cher threw the blazer over the top of the spots and the squares, paring everything back ever so slightly.

So if you're looking to pull off a similar print clash, bear that in mind. It's all about striking the right balance, both with your prints and what you style them with. First of all, what should you pair together? Well, there's no such thing as 'should'. Cher did spots and squares. And actually, leopard is always a good starting point because, as we've seen, it's almost considered a neutral. I personally like mixing leopard-print jeans with a striped jumper of pink and red or black and yellow, using a single-breasted black overcoat to dial down the clash to a level acceptable outside a red-carpet context. Stripes also clash brilliantly with polka dots, particularly if you choose a colour palette of black and white. Also, don't forget that a single pattern can be worn multiple ways to create a clash, for example stripes of contrasting sizes or a blown-up floral next to something more ditsy in nature.

Once you've dabbled, you can go bigger and bolder, mixing prints that are so wrong they're right – think chintz with pinstripes, tartan with tiger, or gingham with polka dots. As long as you incorporate a grounding element to pull it back at the final moment, you'll be fine. Better than fine – you'll look a little bit like Cher.

CONCLUSION

There can't be more than one Cher. But hopefully, by now, you'll feel equipped to emulate her style principles and, perhaps, to push yourself out of your style comfort zone, whether that's with rock 'n' roll leather, a crystallised bodystocking, stacked mule sandals or a combination of all three. Remember: Cher doesn't take her wardrobe too seriously. And if you start to second-guess yourself, wondering if what you're planning to wear is 'appropriate', just remember the immortal words of Cher: 'Snap out of it!'

PICTURE CREDITS

Images kindly provided by: Getty (p.16 Bettmann; p.22 CBS Photo Archive; p.32 Michael Ochs Archives; p.48 Ron Galella; p.55 Andreas Rentz; p.64 Michael Ochs Archives; p.81 Michael Ochs Archives; p.84 Harry Langdon; p.101 UK Press; p.108 Pete Still; p.119 Axelle/Bauer-Griffin; p.122 Vinnie Zuffante; p.131 Getty Images; p.134 Ron Galella; p.150 Vinnie Zuffante; p.155 CBS Photo Archive; p.159 Harry Langdon; p.170 Michael Ochs Archives; p.185 Frazer Harrison) and Unsplash (p.75 top left Taylor Heery, top right Hosein Zanbori, bottom left Good Faces, bottom right Apostolos Vamvouras; p.127 Martin Bammer)

REFERENCES

'Celebration at Caesars.' Cher Scholar (accessed 4 October 2024). https://www.cherscholar.com/celebration-at-caesars/

Galanes, Philip, 'Cher Has Never Been a Huge Cher Fan. But She Loves Being Cher.' *The New York Times* (2018). https://www.nytimes.com/2018/09/04/arts/music/cher-abba-broadway-interview.html

The Late Show with David Letterman. CBS (13 November 1987). https://www.youtube.com/watch?v=7msTqzjZ7PU

Moneta, Caitlan, 'We Interviewed Cher and It Was Everything We Hoped It Would Be.' *FASHION* (13 September 2017). https://fashionmagazine.com/style/gap-cher-fall-2017-campaign/

Weber, Bruce, 'Cher's Next Act.' *The New York Times Magazine* (18 October 1987). https://www.nytimes.com/1987/10/18/magazine/cher-s-next-act.html

Oscars (1986). https://www.youtube.com/watch?v=9ptvz4DGrK4

Vlastnik, Frank and Ross, Laura, *The Art of Bob Mackie* (Simon & Schuster, 2021).

Barbara Walters Special. ABC (11 November 1988). https://www.youtube.com/watch?app=desktop&v=_pLPg1_c2Zk&cbrd=1

Academy Award Acceptance Speech Database (accessed 4 October 2024). https://aaspeechesdb.oscars.org/link/060-3

Mewborn, Brant, 'Cher: All-American Vamp.' *After Dark* (February 1979).

Howard, Josiah, *Cher: Strong Enough* (Plexus, 2013).

'Cher Breaks Down 22 Looks From 1965 to Now | Life in Looks.' *Vogue* (2019). https://www.youtube.com/watch?v=ElSJb6CmS3c

'Cher: 19 Minute Read.' *Time* (17 March 1975). https://time.com/archive/6846716/cher/

Lenker, Mauren Lee, '*The Cher Show*: Bob Mackie takes us inside his designs for the new Broadway musical.' *Entertainment Weekly* (14 November 2018). https://ew.com/theater/cher-show-bob-mackie-designs-broadway/

REFERENCES

The Jennifer Hudson Show (1 May 2024). https://www.youtube.com/watch?v=F79-zodhKLs

Warhol, Andy and Colacello, Bob, 'New Again: Cher.' *Interview* (18 March 1982). https://www.interviewmagazine.com/music/new-again-cher

The Phil Donahue Show. WLWD (1985). https://www.youtube.com/watch?v=ERsKYxuSbic

Tangcay, Jazz, 'Cher's 10 Best Looks of All Time, Hand-Picked by Bob Mackie.' *Variety* (20 May 2021). https://variety.com/lists/chers-10-best-outfits-bob-mackie/chers-if-i-could-turn-back-time-outfit/

'Gypsies, Tramps and Weed', *Will & Grace*. NBC (16 November 2000). https://www.youtube.com/watch?v=mfqC28HcNjk

The Dick Cavett Show. PBS (22 March 1982). https://www.youtube.com/watch?v=mumfjj5-V-I

Woo, Elaine, 'Fred Slatten dies at 92; king of crazy-high heels and platform shoes.' *Los Angeles Times* (23 July 2015). https://www.latimes.com/local/obituaries/la-me-fred-slatten-20150723-story.html

The Sonny & Cher Comedy Hour. CBS (1974). https://www.youtube.com/watch?v=kcLMwIJcIjQ

Display quote sources

Introduction
Cher, *Vogue*. https://www.vogue.co.uk/beauty/article/cher-beauty-looks

Chapter 1
Cher, *Vogue*. https://www.vogue.com/article/cher-best-hair-moments-birthday

Chapter 2
'Costume Designer Bob Mackie Is Back at It With *The Cher Show*.' The Cut (10 January 2019). https://www.thecut.com/article/bob-mackie-the-cher-show.html

Chapter 3
'*The Cher Show*: Bob Mackie takes us inside his designs for the new Broadway musical.' *Entertainment Weekly* (14 November 2018). https://ew.com/theater/cher-show-bob-mackie-designs-broadway/

Chapter 4
Cher interviewed for *Coronet* (1974). Quoted in Howard, Josiah, *Cher: Strong Enough* (Plexus, 2013).

Chapter 5
Cher interviewed for *Wogan* (4 January 1988). https://www.youtube.com/watch?v=nzJj_suagQg

Chapter 6
'Cher Q&A: On her new tour, "sloppy" Miley, and leather jackets.' CNN (24 September 2013). https://edition.cnn.com/2013/09/24/showbiz/music/cher-new-tour/index.html

Chapter 7
'We Interviewed Cher and It Was Everything We Hoped It Would Be.' *FASHION* (13 September 2017). https://fashionmagazine.com/style/gap-cher-fall-2017-campaign/

Chapter 8
'New Again: Cher.' *Interview* (18 March 1982). https://www.interviewmagazine.com/music/new-again-cher

Chapter 9
'Cher Just Doesn't Quit.' *Paper* (26 October 2023). https://www.papermag.com/cher-cover#rebelltitem2

Chapter 10
Cher interviewed for *Dinah!* (12 September 1975). https://www.youtube.com/watch?v=L0GitfSiaww

ACKNOWLEDGEMENTS

Thank you to my peerless editing team, Sam and Emily, for your encouragement and sensitivity at every juncture. Thank you to Jo, for the seamless copyediting. I'm also incredibly grateful to Claire, the designer, and Ollie, the illustrator. Thank you both for bringing the words to life with such flair.

This one felt personal because, to me, Cher is the ultimate in so many respects; not just a trail-blazing style icon, but also a person who lives fearlessly. I hope this book encourages you to believe you can do the same.

ABOUT THE AUTHOR

Natalie Hammond is the senior fashion news editor at *Grazia*. She previously worked on the fashion desk at *The Times*, and her writing has appeared in publications including the *Telegraph*, the *Financial Times* and *gal-dem*. She studied English Literature at the University of Exeter, and has a master's degree in Magazine Journalism from City University. She is also the author of *Bowie: His Style Principles* and *Dolly: Her Style Principles*.

Pop Press

UK | USA | Canada | Ireland | Australia
India | New Zealand | South Africa

Pop Press is part of the Penguin Random House group of companies whose addresses can be found at global.penguinrandomhouse.com

Penguin Random House UK
One Embassy Gardens, 8 Viaduct Gardens, London SW11 7BW

penguin.co.uk
global.penguinrandomhouse.com

First published by Pop Press in 2025

1

© Pop Press 2025

No part of this book may be used or reproduced in any manner for the purpose of training artificial intelligence technologies or systems. In accordance with Article 4(3) of the DSM Directive 2019/790, Penguin Random House expressly reserves this work from the text and data mining exception.

Text: Natalie Hammond
Design: Claire Rochford
Illustrations: Ollie Mann

Printed and bound in Malaysia by Times Offset (M) Sdn Bhd

The authorised representative in the EEA is Penguin Random House Ireland, Morrison Chambers, 32 Nassau Street, Dublin D02 YH68.

A CIP catalogue record for this book is available from the British Library

ISBN 9781529954968

Penguin Random House is committed to a sustainable future for our business, our readers and our planet. This book is made from Forest Stewardship Council® certified paper.